Study Guide

An Introduction to Financial Markets and Institutions

Maureen Burton
California State Polytechnic University – Pomona

Reynold Nesiba
Augustana College

Ray Lombra
Pennsylvania State University – University Park

Prepared by

Francis E. Laatsch
Bowling Green State University

Australia · Canada · Mexico · Singapore · Spain · United Kingdom · United States

Study Guide for *An Introduction to Financial Markets and Institutions*

Maureen Burton, Reynold Nesiba, and Ray Lombra

Editor-in-Chief:
Jack Calhoun

VP/Team Director:
Michael P. Roche

Acquisitions Editor:
Michael R. Reynolds

Senior Developmental Editor:
Susanna C. Smart

Marketing Manager:
Charlie Stutesman

Senior Production Editor:
Kara ZumBahlen

Manufacturing Coordinator:
Sandee Milewski

Printer:
Globus Printing

COPYRIGHT © 2003
by South-Western, a division of Thomson Learning. Thomson Learning™ is a trademark used herein under license.

Printed in the United States of America
1 2 3 4 5 05 04 03 02

ISBN: 0-324-14593-4

ALL RIGHTS RESERVED.
No part of this work covered by the copyright hereon may be reproduced or used in any form or by any means—graphic, electronic, or mechanical, including photocopying, recording, taping, Web distribution or information storage and retrieval systems—without the written permission of the publisher.

For permission to use material from this text or product, contact us by
Tel (800) 730-2214
Fax (800) 730-2215
http://www.thomsonrights.com

For more information
contact South-Western,
5191 Natorp Boulevard,
Mason, Ohio 45040.
Or you can visit our Internet site at:
http://www.swcollege.com

Contents

Part ONE Introduction
Chapter 1: Introduction and Overview 1
Chapter 2: Money: A Unique Financial Instrument 7
Chapter 3: Financial Markets, Instruments, and Market Makers 15
Chapter 4: The Federal Reserve System 23

Part TWO Financial Prices
Chapter 5: Interest Rates and Bond Prices 31
Chapter 6: The Structure of Interest Rates 41
Chapter 7: Market Efficiency 49
Chapter 8: How Exchange Rates Are Determined 57

Part THREE Financial Markets and Instruments
Chapter 9: The Money Market 65
Chapter 10: The Corporate and Government Bond Markets 73
Chapter 11: The Stock Market 81
Chapter 12: The Mortgage Market 91
Chapter 13: The International Financial System 99

Part FOUR Financial Institutions
Chapter 14: An Introduction to Financial Intermediaries and Risk 107
Chapter 15: Commercial Banking Structure, Regulation, and Performance ... 113
Chapter 16: Savings Associations and Credit Unions 121
Chapter 17: Regulation of the Banking and Financial Services Industry 127
Chapter 18: Insurance Companies 135
Chapter 19: Pension Plans and Finance Companies 143
Chapter 20: Securities Firms, Mutual Funds, and Financial Conglomerates .. 151

Part FIVE Managing Financial Risk
Chapter 21: Risk Assessment and Management 159
Chapter 22: Forward, Futures, and Options Agreements 167
Chapter 23: Asset-Backed Securities, Interest Rate Agreements,
and Currency Swaps 175

Part SIX Monetary Policy
Chapter 24: Monetary Policy and the Financial System 181
Chapter 25: Monetary Policy in a Globalized Financial System 187
Answers 193

Introduction and Overview

SUMMARY

1. Finance is closely related to economics. Indeed, a more fully descriptive name for finance is financial economics. Most students will have had at least one economics class prior to reading this text. It's important that you review the major issues studied in economics – allocation of scarce resources, income distribution, and consumption versus savings and investment.

2. The concepts of a deficit spending unit (DSU), i.e., a borrower, and a surplus spending unit (SSU), i.e., a saver/lender, are fundamental to the study of financial markets and institutions. Financial markets and institutions exist to more efficiently connect DSUs and SSUs. DSUs have a need for funds that exceed their current income. Think of businesses that are expanding, building new plants or launching new products or services. SSUs, in contrast, are willing to consume less than their current income. Think of households that wish to save for down payments on houses. The foregone consumption is called savings. SSUs invest, through one mechanism or another, these savings into financial assets issued by DSUs.

3. Financial markets provide a venue for the efficient trading of financial assets. Financial assets (think of stocks and bonds, for the most part) are assets that provide the SSUs that buy the assets with a claim on the future income of the DSUs that issue the financial assets. Financial assets, then, are claims on future income. Financial assets trade more efficiently in specialized financial markets for much the same reasons that produce and canned goods trade more efficiently through your local grocery store than through direct mail. Consumers recognize that grocery stores specialize in selling food. Consumers go there when they want to buy food. Farmers and producers find it much easier to sell to a relatively small number of grocery stores than to try and sell door-to-door directly to consumers. Similarly, DSUs find that it is easier to sell stocks and bonds to SSUs through financial markets and the financial institutions that operate in financial markets (think of banks, brokerage houses, insurance companies, etc.) rather than solicit funds from SSUs by going door-to-door.

4. In analyzing the attractiveness of a particular financial asset, SSUs are concerned with the potential reward (increased future consumption) *and* the potential risk (the possibility of default, among other risks). Finance almost never concerns itself solely with return, or solely with risk. Financial decisions are virtually always a tradeoff of return versus risk. The nature of the tradeoff is clear – in order to get SSUs to accept higher risk investments, the investments must offer a higher (expected or on-average) reward. Risk and reward are positively related.

5. Direct finance means DSUs receive funds directly from SSUs, although a broker, who specializes in seeking out willing SSUs and needy DSUs, often brings the two together. Indirect finance involves the use of true financial intermediaries. The term financial intermediary is often loosely used to refer to any function that brings SSUs and DSUs together. A true financial intermediary, however, creates a new financial asset that SSUs have a future claim against. For example, an investor might buy stock in General Motors – this is direct finance as the investor has a direct claim against GM. On the other hand, an investor might place money into a bank savings account. The bank might then lend the money to GM. The bank has created a financial asset – a savings account – that the investor has a claim against. The investor (the SSU) has no direct claim on GM, even though his or her savings eventually flowed through the bank to GM.

6. The most important financial intermediaries – in the strict sense of the term intermediary – are depository institutions (i.e., institutions that have savings and checking accounts) such as commercial banks, savings and loan associations, mutual savings banks, and credit unions. Important intermediaries among non-depository institutions are life and casualty insurance companies, pension funds, mutual funds and money market mutual funds, and finance companies.

7. The role of the Federal Reserve banks, the scope and function of other financial regulators, and the effectiveness (or ineffectiveness) of economic policy decisions are important parts of the study of financial markets and institutions. Later chapters devote significant coverage to these topics.

TRUE/FALSE QUESTIONS

T F 1. In financial economics, individuals who spend more than their current income are known as Surplus Spending Units (SSUs).

T F 2. The formation of new capital goods is designed to generate greater future consumption possibilities, but, holding all other factors constant, it necessarily imposes the cost of reduced current consumption.

T F 3. Given the success of deregulation in the 1980's, most U.S. economists have embraced a laissez-faire approach to economics in which the federal government has almost no regulatory functions.

T F 4. Indirect finance requires a financial intermediary to connect SSUs to DSUs.

T F 5. Financial assets represent a claim on a portion of the future income of the entity issuing the financial asset.

T F 6. The United States Treasury Department performs most of the nation's central banking functions, although United States currency is currently only issued in the form of Federal Reserve Notes.

T F 7. In general, when SSUs lend to DSUs through a financial intermediary such as a commercial bank, the SSUs face less risk of not recovering their investment because of a default by a DSU.

T F   8. Because financial intermediaries impose transactions cost on financial markets, it is generally more attractive for DSUs to seek out SSUs through direct mail campaigns or other such mechanisms that "eliminate the middleman." F

T F   9. Depository institutions, such as commercial banks, allow withdrawal of money from checking accounts "on demand." However, once deposited, it is never possible to withdraw funds from non-depository institutions such as pension funds or insurance companies. F

T F   10. Deregulation of the financial markets has allowed for more competition among financial institutions to the point where it is now not always possible to clearly distinguish commercial banks from insurance companies, to give just one example. T

T F   11. One nice thing about the study of economics is that economists generally are able to form clear and unquestioned policy recommendations whose impact is fully understood by all participants in the economy. F

T F   12. Prior to the Great Depression of the 1930's, the United States federal government engaged in relatively little regulation of financial markets or institutions. T

T F   13. From the perspective of the typical individual, finance essentially boils down to making payments on time and managing funds efficiently until they are needed. T

T F   14. Business firms can only be DSUs. F

T F   15. For the most part, stock brokerage firms do not act as financial intermediaries. T

T F   16. Liquidity refers simply to the ease of exchanging a financial asset for cash. More liquid assets can be more quickly changed into cash. T

T F   17. Holding all else constant, the higher the proportion of income devoted to consumption, the easier it will be to create new capital goods. F

T F   18. It is generally illegal for United States depository institutions to pay interest on checking accounts. F

T F   19. Checkable deposits cannot be considered money. F

MULTIPLE CHOICE QUESTIONS

1. If one's income exceeds one's consumption, the difference:
   a. by definition, is savings
   b. can be used to purchase financial assets
   c. can be used to reduce one's outstanding indebtedness
   d. a, b, and c above
   e. none of the above as, by definition, income can never exceed consumption

   D

2. Financial intermediaries include all of the following except:
   a. commercial banks
   b. stock brokers
   c. credit unions
   d. life insurance companies
   e. property and casualty insurance companies

3. Which of the following activities indicate that the business firm was a SSU for the period of time in which the activity occurred?
   a. the firm reduced its total indebtedness without issuing new equity (new stock)
   b. the credit rating of the firm's bonds increased
   c. the firm increased the dividend it paid on its common stock
   d. all of the above

4. An economic environment wherein the government imposes little regulatory burden on producers and provides little protection for consumers is referred to as:
   a. laissez-faire
   b. voulez le bon temps roulez
   c. les miserables
   d. caveat emptor
   e. Gemuetlichkeit

5. Financial assets (financial instruments):
   a. are issued by SSUs and purchased by DSUs
   b. are claims on the future income of SSUs
   c. generally offer higher potential rewards as compensation if they also have a greater possibility of default
   d. all of the above
   e. none of the above

6. You purchase shares issued by a mutual fund. This is an example of:
   a. a mistake
   b. direct finance
   c. indirect finance
   d. a demand deposit

7. All of the following describe elements of the business cycle except:
   a. expansion
   b. recession
   c. contraction
   d. intercession

8. In evaluating the attractiveness of investing in financial assets, SSUs consider:
   a. expected return
   b. liquidity
   c. the risk of loss
   d. a and c only
   e. all of the above

9. The fastest growing economy, holding all other factors constant, is most likely to be one in which
   a. all participants are DSUs
   b. all participants are SSUs
   c. the flow of funds from SSUs to DSUs is regulated by setting strict interest rate ceilings
   d. a variety of choices exist that allow the flow of funds from SSUs to DSUs

10. When SSUs participate in indirect financing:
    a. they forego all claims on any financial asset
    b. they have a claim on the financial asset issued by a financial intermediary
    c. DSUs never receive the money
    d. all of the above
    e. none of the above

FILL IN QUESTIONS

1. SSUs have income that _____ their consumption, while DSUs have income that _____ their consumption.

2. The role of the central bank in the United States economy is played by the _____.

3. One is most likely to observe the highest unemployment at the _____ of the business cycle.

4. In comparison to the 1960s, unemployment in the 1970s was _____ while inflation rates were _____.

5. In evaluating the attractiveness of investing in a financial asset, SSUs should consider both the asset's _____ and its _____.

ESSAY QUESTIONS

1. Place yourself in the position of advising a poor nation as to the best means to achieve economic growth. You are convinced that such growth will require a significant increase in investment in capital goods. However, you observe that virtually all of the residents of the nation live at a bare subsistence level. How can this nation increase its savings rate so as to fund the needed investments in capital goods? What alternative means exist to fund the needed investments? Should market forces alone guide such savings and investment decisions, or should such decisions be based on humanitarian grounds? Is it humanitarian to burden an impoverished nation with debt and its associated future financial payments? What role can international financial markets play in the development of the country? [By the way, if you are able to give a definitive and complete answer to these questions, you should consider immediately applying for the job of Administrator of the U.S. Agency for International Development or a similar post!]

2. Is it possible for a nation with a very high savings rate to nonetheless experience low growth in the formation of new capital goods? Is it possible for a nation with a very low savings rate to experience rapid growth in the formation of productive capital goods? Could one or both of these scenarios be sustained over the long-term?

3. What does "ceteris paribus" mean?

INTERNET EXERCISES

1. Visit the International Monetary Fund Web site at http://www.imf.org. Click on the "World Economic Outlook" link. Download the chapter on world economic prospects. What stage of the business cycle do the staff economists of the IMF think the world is currently in? Do different parts of the world appear to be in different stages of the business cycle?

2. Go to the Ohio State University Virtual Finance Library at http://fisher.osu.edu/fin/overview.htm. Click on the "For Students" link. Try out the "Iowa Electronic Markets" link. Want to try your luck on predicting future political activities? For real money? Then this is the place.

2

Money: A Unique Financial Instrument

SUMMARY

1. Money is what money does – and what money does is threefold. First, money serves as a generally acceptable means of payment (medium of exchange). Second, money is a store of value; that is, money retains its value, at least over fairly short periods of time. Third, money serves as a unit of account; that is, other goods and services are priced in units of money. In the United States, the unit of account is the dollar. Apples are not priced in units of oranges, nor are hamburgers priced in units of kumquats. All goods (except for the rare barter transaction) are priced in units of dollars.

2. Barter (i.e., non-monetary exchange of one physical good for another) requires a "double coincidence of wants." If you have three quarts of milk to sell and are in need of some turpentine to clean your paintbrushes, to engage in a successful barter you need to be lucky enough to bump into a fellow who just happens to have a gallon of turpentine for sale and needs three quarts of milk. Not very likely! Money-based transactions are obviously dramatically more efficient than wandering about looking for such double coincidences.

3. Measuring the amount of money in the economy is not easy. However, knowing the amount of money in the economy is an important clue for policymakers. Money creation (and destruction) is related to economic growth, even if the relationship is often inconsistent from one period to the next. It seems especially difficult to understand the variations in the lags between changes in the money supply and related economic changes. Nonetheless, in general terms, supply and demand determine the price of money much as supply and demand determine the price of most economic goods. The price of money is the interest rate. When demand for money is high relative to the supply of money, interest rates rise. Conversely, when supply is high relative to demand, interest rates fall. The actions of the Federal Reserve impact supply (and to a lesser extent, demand) for money and thus influence (and some say determine) interest rates. It is therefore important to understand how the Fed measures money.

4. The Federal Reserve uses four estimates of money. The four measures are: M1, M2, M3, and DNFD (domestic nonfinancial debt). M1 consists of coin, currency, and checkable deposits. Checkable deposits are the major component of M1. All three elements of M1 are available for immediate transactions; thus, M1 is closest to the definition of money as an acceptable means of payment. M2 adds savings accounts and individual money market funds to M1. These additional components are not as liquid as checking accounts or currency. Still, you can write a limited number of checks per month on your money market mutual fund. And some savings institutions issue debit cards that access savings accounts. Indeed, if savings account debit cards grow in popularity, the Fed may

choose to redefine M1 to include some portion of these savings accounts, which simply shows that all these definitions do change over time. M3 consists of everything in M2 plus large time deposits, some Eurodollar and repurchase agreements, as well as institutional money market funds. Domestic nonfinancial debt (DNFD) consists of all the debt outstanding in the economy except the debt issued by financial institutions.

5. One rather nervous species of economists, *economicus fedwatcherii*, spends most of its time watching for Federal Reserve changes in monetary policy. Fed watchers are trying to guess if the Fed is about to lower or raise interest rates or increase or decrease the supply of money. Watching the Fed is difficult because the monetary rules the Fed uses change in response to changing economic conditions. For example, during the 1980s, the Fed targeted M1, and later M2, in an attempt to keep the economy growing with inflation under control. By the 1990s, the relationship between M1 and M2 and interest rates, growth, and inflation became erratic. Thus, the Fed began to use growth in DNFD as its most important measure. But DNFD's relationship to economic aggregates also proved erratic, so now the Fed uses a set of indicators (including perhaps tea leaves and consultations with the Delphic oracle?) to guide policy.

6. Credit flows (loans) impact aggregate income, consumption, savings, etc. If interest rates are low, for example, it will be easier to finance the purchase of a house or car. And if interest rates are low, it will be less attractive to place money into a savings account, etc. Ceteris paribus (i.e., holding all other factors the same), lower rates should stimulate consumption and reduce savings. Higher rates will have opposite effects. However, it turns out in the real world it is very difficult to keep all those ceterii (things) paribused (kept equal), to coin a phrase.

TRUE/FALSE QUESTIONS

T F   1. Any good or service that can be exchanged for another good or service qualifies as money. F

T F   2. Money possesses the very attractive quality that it can never decline in value. F

T F   3. In the United States, most money – as money is defined in M1 – is held in the form of currency. F

T F   4. More than half of all United States currency is actually held by individuals and institutions that reside outside of United States territory. T

T F   5. Under a reserve banking system, banks are able to lend out only a portion of the deposits that investors place into the banking system. T

T F   6. The Federal Reserve has substantially more control over the supply of money than it has over the demand for money. T

T F   7. Holding all other factors constant (the famous "ceteris paribus" conditions), higher interest rates generate increased demand for money. F

T F   8. For a given supply of money, a reduction in the demand for money will result in falling interest rates. T

Chapter 2 — Money: A Unique Financial Instrument

T F 9. In managing U.S. monetary policy, the Federal Reserve has learned over the past three decades that credit flows from SSUs outside of the United States have essentially no effect on U.S. interest rates. F

T F 10. A sustained and significant rise in the money supply and credit growth rates will, with a lag of uncertain duration, tend to reduce the rate of inflation. F

T F 11. A sustained and significant rise in the money supply and credit growth rates will tend to raise aggregate demand for goods and services. T

T F 12. Historically, the Federal Reserve has exerted greater influence on commercial banks than on other financial institutions. Thus, as the market share that commercial banks have in financial transactions falls, the ability of the Federal Reserve to direct monetary policy is reduced. T

T F 13. M1 refers to financial assets that possess only the "unit of account" feature of money, while M2 instruments possess both the "unit of account" and the "store of value" features. Only financial instruments belonging to M3 possess all three feature of money – unit of account, store of value, and medium of exchange. F

T F 14. M1 consists of currency, traveler's checks, and all commercial bank deposits. F

T F 15. Domestic nonfinancial debt (DNFD) consists of all debts currently owed by all U.S. entities. F

T F 16. The price of money is the interest rate. T

T F 17. In the abstract, financial economists speak of the interest rate (singular) but actually have in mind the set of interest rates (plural) that exist at any one time in the economy. T

T F 18. Whenever aggregate demand for goods and services increases, there is a general tendency for output to rise (relatively) quickly and for prices to rise more gradually. T

T F 19. Savings accounts cannot be considered money. F

T F 20. If an expansion of the money supply actually causes interest rates, especially long-term interest rates, to rise rather than fall, it is an indicator that market participants fear an increase in inflation. T

T F 21. Money is itself a commodity and thus it responds to changes in supply and demand in much the same way as do other commodities. T

T F 22. If the Federal Reserve were to increase the required reserve ratio, this would most likely increase both M1 and M2, but have little effect on M3. F

T F 23. In equilibrium, neither supply nor demand exists. F

T F 24. The term "credit flows" refers to the movement of funds from SSUs to DSUs in the form of new loans as well as flows from DSUs to SSUs that repay previous loans. T

T F   25. Under existing U.S. laws and regulations, credit cards may only be issued by depository institutions such as commercial banks.   F

MULTIPLE CHOICE QUESTIONS

1. By definition, money possesses all of the following characteristics except: c
   a. it is a store of value
   b. it is a medium of exchange
   c. it is only created by the actions of a central bank
   d. it is a unit of account

2. In the typical graphical presentation of the demand for money and the supply of money (see Exhibit 2-7 in the text), the supply of money is depicted as a straight vertical line. This is because: A
   a. at any given point in time, there is a fixed supply of money
   b. the supply of money expands exponentially with changes in interest rates
   c. the supply of money expands linearly with changes in interest rates
   d. the supply of money is highly elastic

3. Keeping in mind that the most important feature of money is that it is accepted as a means of payment, the monetary aggregate that most closely corresponds to this sense of money is: A
   a. M1
   b. M2
   c. M3
   d. DNFD

4. Historically, as the economy grows, the demand for money also grows. If the Federal Reserve were to keep the supply of money constant in the face of this increased demand: A
   a. interest rates would most likely rise
   b. interest rates would also likely remain constant
   c. interest rates would most likely fall
   d. the economy would grow faster

5. If M1 is rising, but M2 is falling and M3 is little changed: C
   a. the Fed will always focus on the change in M1
   b. the Fed will probably use DNFD as its primary guide
   c. the Fed will have difficulty saying if the money supply is rising or falling
   d. the Fed will defer to the Treasury in establishing monetary policy

6. If demand for money were to increase, but the supply of money were also to increase, the effect on interest rates would be: B
   a. to increase interest rates
   b. difficult to determine without more precise information
   c. to reduce interest rates

Chapter 2 Money: A Unique Financial Instrument

d. negligible

7. A double coincidence of wants:
   a. occurs when two people want the same asset at the same time
   b. occurs when the goods I have for sale exactly match the goods you desire to buy
   c. occurs when the goods I desire to buy exactly match the goods you have for sale
   d. requires b and c to happen simultaneously

8. M3 contains all of the following except:
   a. currency
   b. money market mutual funds
   c. corporate bonds
   d. checkable deposits
   e. all of the above are included in M3

9. M2 can be described as:
   a. currency, demand deposits, other checkable deposits, traveler's checks, small savings and time deposits, and individual money market mutual funds
   b. M1 plus small savings and time deposits and individual money market mutual funds
   c. money and near monies
   d. all of the above
   e. none of the above

10. Technological advancements have changed the transfer of payments mechanism in which of the following ways?
    a. neutron regeneration machines
    b. stored value cards
    c. deep introspect banking systems
    d. b and c

11. Domestic nonfinancial debt (DNFD) contains:
    a. U.S. municipal bonds
    b. U.S federal government debt
    c. U.S. consumer debt
    d. commercial paper issued by nonfinancial firms
    e. all of the above

12. The economic concept of equilibrium:
    a. holds when there is no excess supply at a given price
    b. holds when there is no excess demand at a given price
    c. can never hold, even in approximation
    d. must include both a and b

13. The possibility that money might lose its store of value quality is more commonly referred to as the threat of:
    a. interdiction
    b. introspection
    c. inculcation
    d. inflation

14. Demand deposits are distinguished from checkable deposits in that:

11

a. demand deposits pay no interest
b. checkable deposits function as money, but demand deposits do not
c. demand deposits can be withdrawn through ATMs, but checkable deposits can not be withdrawn from ATMs
d. demand deposits are part of M2, but checkable deposits are not

15. If the Federal Reserve were to increase the required reserve ratio, holding all other factors constant:
    a. interest rates would be more likely to fall than rise
    b. the money supply would likely increase
    c. the amount of loans outstanding would likely increase
    d. all of the above
    e. none of the above

16. Each of the following meets the definition of money except:
    a. U.S. $20 Federal Reserve note
    b. Bank of England £5 note
    c. VISA credit card
    d. American Express $50 traveler's check

17. Nondepository institutions such as Sears and General Motors have begun to engage in activities once exclusive to depository institutions. Among these are:
    a. mortgage loans
    b. credit cards
    c. consumer loans
    d. all of the above

18. If it waddles like a duck, and quacks like a duck:
    a. it is a duck
    b. it might nonetheless be a goose
    c. it is one of the dumbest things any U.S politician (it was George Bush the elder's budget director) has ever said, but still a memorable way to state that a tax, even if not called a tax, is still a tax
    d. it will make for a very nice roast
    e. a, c, and d

FILL IN QUESTIONS

1. A change in the quantity demanded indicates movement _____ the demand curve, while a change in demand indicates movement _____ the demand curve.

2. Money has three characteristics: (1) _____, (2) _____, and (3) _____.

3. The difficult (if not impossible) task of finding a "double coincidence of wants" exists in _____ -based economies.

4. "Near monies" include both _____ and _____.

5. If your employer automatically deposits your paycheck into your bank, you are participating in the _____ _____ _____ system.

6. The specific amount of money that spending units wish to hold at a specific interest rate is the definition of _____.

7. The proportion of deposits that banks and other financial institutions must hold in reserve is set by the Federal Reserve and is known as the _____ _____ _____.

8. The _____ curve is downward sloping, indicating that when interest rates are high, the amount of money _____ is low.

9. The Federal Reserve relied on _____ to guide monetary policy during the early 1980s. By the latter half of that decade, the Fed's emphasis had switched to _____. In the early 1990s, the Fed began to use _____ to guide policy decisions.

10. A sustained fall in the money supply and credit growth rates will tend to _____ aggregate demand, _____ output growth, and, after a time, _____ the inflation rate.

ESSAY QUESTIONS

1. Demonstrate, using simple graphical flow charts such as that seen in Exhibit 2-9 in the text, why including the debt issued by financial institutions in DNFD would "double count" such debt.

2. Suppose you know for certain that if the Federal Reserve announces a large increase in M1, the economy will begin to grow far more quickly than its current rate of growth. Thousands more Americans will have jobs, be able to afford cars and houses, be better able to care for their elderly relatives, etc. Unfortunately, you are also chief economist of the Fed and you know for an actual fact that M1 growth over the most recent reporting period was flat to a slight decline. Should you report the actual M1 figure or should you tell "a little white lie" in order to give the economy the boost it needs?

3. U.S. consumers appear to be hoarding the new "Sacajawea" dollar coin, saving the coins in glass jars or in their clothes drawers rather than spending them. However, they do not appear to hoard dollar bills. Why? (Hint: look up the word "numismatic.") If the government continues to mint thousands of the new coin, will consumers stop hoarding these coins?

INTERNET EXERCISES

1. Visit the Federal Reserve Board of Governors Web site - http://www.federalreserve.gov. In particular, look at the Fed's policy Web site -http://www.federalreserve.gov/policy.htm. What does the site tell you about the current monetary policy stance of the Federal Reserve? Read through the latest "Beige Book" report at http://www.federalreserve.gov/FOMC/BeigeBook. Now write down what U.S. monetary policy is. (Hint: don't be surprised if after reading the "Beige Book" you still are not quite sure what U.S. policy is).

2. The United States' largest trading partner is Canada. Go to - http://www.bankofcanada.ca/en/histor.htm – the Web site of the Bank of Canada, to read a short history of the central bank of Canada. Link to the Bank of Canada's monetary policy Web site - http://www.bankofcanada.ca/en/monetary.htm. Contrast the Bank of Canada's presentation of its monetary policy goals to those presented at the Federal Reserve site referenced above. Do the two nations have differing policy goals? Which Web site presented the information in an easier to understand format? Link to the section "How Monetary Policy Works" - http://www.bankofcanada.ca/en/monetary/index.htm - and work through the presentation.

3. E-money and its equivalents will surely grow in importance over the next decades. The Bank for International Settlements addresses this issue at http://www.bis.org/publ/cpss38.htm. Take a look to learn the pluses and minuses of electronic payments.

3

Financial Markets, Instruments, and Market Makers

SUMMARY

1. As noted in the opening paragraphs of this chapter, knowing the "jargon" used is important in any endeavor. The essence of this chapter is knowing the following terms: the money market versus the capital market, primary markets versus secondary markets, spot markets versus forward and futures markets, and market makers.

2. The money market is where securities with original maturities of one year or less are traded. Money market instruments include Treasury bills (note: bills, but *not* notes nor bonds). T-bills are short-term debt instruments of the U.S. government. T-bills are very safe as it is inconceivable that the U.S. government will default on its obligations. If conditions ever were to seriously threaten repayment of its debts, the U.S. government is in the unique position of being able to create money out of thin air and use that money to pay its debts. Bad things might happen as the government increases the money supply in this way, but not as bad as those that would happen were the government to default. The T-bill market is also very liquid with millions of dollars of T-bills trading on a typical day. You must also know T-bills are "pure discount" instruments. They do not pay dividends or coupons. One purchases a T-bill at some price less than par value (that is, at a discount) and receives par value at maturity. T-bills are quoted using "discount yields." These discount yields are given in annual terms and must be adjusted for bills with maturities of less than one year (which is to say, for all T-bills). Chapter 9 discusses discount yields and T-bill prices in greater detail.

3. Other money market instruments include negotiable CDs, commercial paper, bankers' acceptances, repurchase agreements, fed funds, and Eurodollars.

4. The capital market is where securities with original maturities of more than one year are traded. Instruments traded in the capital markets include stocks (both common and preferred), mortgages, corporate bonds, U.S. Treasury notes and Treasury bonds, and other government bonds.

5. Primary markets are where new securities are first sold to the public. Chapter 20 covers primary market operations in more detail. Secondary markets are where existing securities are bought and sold and are also discussed in more detail in Chapter 20. Without well-developed secondary markets,

Chapter 3   Financial Markets, Instruments, and Market Makers

where one can easily sell securities for a fair value, it would be difficult to convince SSUs to purchase securities in the primary market.

6. Spot or cash markets are markets for immediate delivery. Forward and futures markets offer the opportunity for buyers and sellers to negotiate an acceptable price, but delivery of the goods is to occur, at that price, sometime in the future. Chapter 22 discusses these markets in greater detail.

7. Market makers stand ready to buy from and/or sell to the public the securities they make a market in. Market makers buy and sell from inventory. Like all dealers, they try to buy from the public at one price (the bid price) and sell back to the public at a slightly higher price (the ask, or offer, price).

TRUE/FALSE QUESTIONS

T F 1. Money markets are those markets where monies issued by differing governments worldwide are traded.   F

T F 2. Treasury bills, notes, and bonds all trade in the money market. *Capital Market*   F

T F 3. DSU's do not receive funds from secondary market trading in the securities the DSUs have previously issued in the primary market.   T

T F 4. In both futures and forward markets goods are delivered immediately, but the price at which they are delivered is not determined until a future date. *Price now, Del later*   F

T F 5. Market makers set both the bid and ask prices. Bid prices tend to be higher, on average, than ask prices. *Bid < Ask*   F

T F 6. The primary market is analogous to the new car market, while the secondary market is analogous to the used car market.   T

T F 7. An asset that can be quickly turned into cash, provided that a large reduction in price is accepted by the seller, is a liquid asset.   F

T F 8. At any one point in time, the bid price for a Treasury bill is lower than the ask price for that same Treasury bill.   T

T F 9. Eurodollars are simply U.S. dollars, but those dollars are deposited in banks outside of the United States.   T

T F 10. By far, in U.S. capital markets, the single largest component of the capital market is corporate stock.   F

T F 11. Primary market trading in corporate stock exceeds secondary market trading in corporate stock on the typical trading day.   F

T F 12. The typical residential mortgage would trade in the money market. *Capital*   F

16

Chapter 3 — Financial Markets, Instruments, and Market Makers

T F 13. Securities brokers always buy and sell from the inventory they carry, but securities dealers never do. F

T F 14. Interest payments on many of the bonds issued by state and local governments are exempt from Federal income tax. This reduced tax burden makes these bonds particularly attractive to retired individuals living on modest pensions. F

T F 15. There is no real difference between Eurodollars and Euros. F

T F 16. Periodic payments made to stockholders are called dividends, while periodic payments made to bondholders are known as coupon payments. T

T F 17. If a recession were to become severe enough, as in the Great Depression of the 1930s, the possibility that the U.S. Treasury will default on its debt obligations would become frighteningly real. F

T F 18. Spot markets allow for delivery "on the spot" (i.e., now), whereas futures markets allow for delivery in the future. However, prices, in both markets, are determined now. T

T F 19. Although the various ways of classifying financial markets into submarkets suggests that these markets are separate entities, in reality these submarkets are well connected and more alike than different. T

T F 20. DSUs receive funds from the sale of securities to SSUs only in primary market transactions. Therefore, DSUs are unconcerned with secondary market trading of these securities. F

T F 21. For almost every U.S. financial submarket, corresponding markets can be found in developed nations such as Japan, the United Kingdom, and Switzerland. T

T F 22. Money market instruments may be sold prior to maturity, but capital market instruments must be held to maturity in order to recover the initial investment placed in the instrument. F

T F 23. If returns in one market, say the municipal bond market, are sufficiently high, many investors that generally only invest in another market, say corporate bonds, will sell the lower yielding assets and begin to buy the higher return assets. T

T F 24. Market makers make markets, pure and simple. They do not give advice nor provide information to their customers. F

T F 25. Futures contracts are standardized and trade on organized exchanges while forward contracts are not standardized and trade among banks and other dealers. T

MULTIPLE CHOICE QUESTIONS

1. All of the following instruments would trade in the capital market except:
    a. mortgages
    b. bankers' acceptances
    c. corporate stock
    d. corporate bonds

    B

2. United States Treasury bills possess all the following features except:
    a. safety
    b. liquidity
    c. high returns
    d. low risk
    e. pure discount instruments

    C

3. Market makers perform all the following functions except:
    a. maintain a smoothly functioning, orderly market
    b. carry an inventory of securities
    c. sell securities to customers
    d. act as agents of their customers when purchasing securities
    e. disseminate information to customers

    D

4. All of the following instruments would trade in the money market except:
    a. Treasury bills
    b. Treasury bonds
    c. negotiable certificates of deposit
    d. bankers' acceptances
    e. repurchase agreements

    B

5. Thirty year mortgages on residential property in the United Kingdom trade on:
    a. the foreign exchange market
    b. the money market
    c. the forward market
    d. the capital market
    e. the housing market

    D

6. Money market mutual funds invest in financial assets such as:
    a. negotiable certificates of deposit
    b. Treasury bonds
    c. money (i.e., coin and currency)
    d. foreign exchange
    e. all of the above

    A

18

7. Which of the following correctly presents the ranking of the financial assets from most liquid to least liquid?
   a. Treasury bonds, Treasury bills, corporate stock, commercial paper
   b. corporate stock, Treasury bonds, commercial paper, Treasury bills
   c. commercial paper, Treasury bonds, Treasury bills, corporate stock
   d. Treasury bills, commercial paper, Treasury bonds, corporate stock
   e. none of the above

8. You open a savings account with a Canadian bank, but your account is denominated in U.S. dollars. Of the following choices, which best and most completely describes your account:
   a. a money market mutual fund
   b. a Eurodollar account
   c. a capital market account
   d. a demand deposit account

9. Financial futures and forwards markets fulfill two basic functions:
   a. speculation and risk transfer (hedging)
   b. gambling and forecasting
   c. wealth creation and wealth destruction
   d. consideration and retribution
   e. matched orders and out trades

10. Fill in the blanks appropriately to best complete the following sentence. "During the 1990s, SSUs removed funds from _____ and increased their ownership of _____."
    a. mortgages; residential property
    b. their cash hoards; gold
    c. savings; commodities
    d. depository institutions; mutual funds

11. Which of the following instruments are included in M3 (M3 was discussed in Chapter 2)?
    a. Treasury bills
    b. commercial paper
    c. bankers' acceptances
    d. corporate bonds
    e. none of the above

12. All of the following function as financial market makers except:
    a. Morgan Stanley (formerly Morgan Stanley Dean Witter)
    b. Merrill Lynch
    c. Goldman Sachs
    d. Johnson & Johnson
    e. Salomon Smith Barney

13. Commercial paper issued in New York by the Paris based bank Societe Generale would be best characterized as being part of the:
    a. capital market
    b. money market
    c. foreign exchange market
    d. Eurodollar market

Chapter 3   Financial Markets, Instruments, and Market Makers

14. Important functions performed by market makers include all of the following except:
    a. they provide financial services that determine the quality of primary and secondary markets
    b. they disseminate information about market conditions to buyers and sellers
    c. they approve or disapprove the appointment by the President of the Chairman of the Board of Governors of the Federal Reserve (under the "advise and consent" clause of the U.S. Constitution)
    d. they connect the various markets by buying and selling in the market themselves

FILL IN QUESTIONS

1. Capital market U.S. government securities issued by the U.S. Treasury have had initial maturities up to _____.

2. Two types of state and local government bonds exist. _____ bonds are backed by the full faith and credit of the issuer. However, _____ bonds only have claim to the specific revenues generated by the project financed by the bonds.

3. Securities are first issued in the _____ market and subsequently trade in the _____ market.

4. Long-lived financial assets trade in the _____ market, while those with maturities of less than one year trade in the _____ market.

5. A financial asset whose potential outcomes are more variable is often described as having greater risk. However, most investors are likely to think of risk as not just variation, per se, but think of risk as being the possibility that the value of the asset will _____.

6. A _____ is a debt instrument sold by a depository institution with a minimum denomination of $100,000 and which has an active secondary market.

7. _____ are dollar-denominated deposits held in banks outside the United States.

8. In order for market makers to make money, they set the _____ price to be higher than the _____ price.

ESSAY QUESTIONS

1. Market makers buy securities from the public at the bid price and sell securities to the public at the ask price. Given this fact, explain why, in the Cracking the Code feature in the chapter discussing Treasury bills, the values shown under the bid column are greater than those under the asked column.

2. How do Euros differ from Eurodollars?

3. Why did the U.S. federal government consider it necessary to sponsor agencies such as Fannie Mae and Ginnie Mae? Wouldn't private investors find mortgages sufficiently attractive investments on their own merits? (Hint: when interest rates go up, existing fixed rate mortgages fall in value, but when interest rates fall, what happens?)

4. When you buy a used 1997 Dodge from a used car dealer, how much of the money you pay for the car goes to Daimler-Chrysler? Carry the analogy to securities markets and discuss (1) why DSUs only receive funds on the sale of securities in the primary market, but (2) they (DSUs) nonetheless remain very interested in the viability of the secondary market.

5. Why is the following statement true? "Virtually every asset can be turned into cash quickly, but that doesn't mean it has high liquidity."

INTERNET EXERCISES

1. Go to the J.P. Morgan Web site - http://www.jpmorgan.com. Check out the investment banking services Morgan offers by clicking on the "Investment Bank" link. Then look at their "Treasury and Securities Services," "Asset Management," and other functions. Click on "Careers" to see if you might find employment with Morgan.

2. Salomon Smith Barney has another interesting web site - http://www.salomonsmithbarney.com. Click on "Institutional Services" and then select "Fixed Income." Salomon is a major player in primary market debt offerings. Click on "Career Center" and perhaps you can find an even better job at Salomon than you found above at Morgan.

4

The Federal Reserve System

SUMMARY

1. The Federal Reserve acts as the U.S. central bank. The Fed is also the most important regulator in U.S financial markets. Perhaps most importantly, the Fed designs and implements U.S. monetary policy. The Federal Reserve System was created by Congress in 1913 and given further responsibilities under the Banking Reform Acts of 1933 and 1935.

2. Under these laws, the Fed has two major purposes – (1) to foster a smooth-running, efficient, and competitive financial system and (2) to promote the overall health and stability of the economy through its ability to influence the cost and availability of money and credit.

3. The Federal Reserve System consists of twelve districts, each with its own Reserve Bank. However, the Board of Governors, located in Washington, D.C., determines monetary policy (in conjunction with the Federal Open Market Committee) and has, essentially, all the regulatory power. The Board has seven members. They are appointed by the President with the advice and consent of the U.S. Senate. The members serve one fourteen-year term with one member elected every two years. The long tenure was designed to insulate the Fed, to some degree, from political pressure as a President, in theory, could only appoint two Board members in a four-year Presidential term.

4. The Chair of the Board of Governors of the Federal Reserve is the most powerful member of the Fed. The Chair and the Vice-Chair are appointed by the President with the advice and consent of the Senate to four-year terms. The Chair is the chief spokesperson for the Fed, sets the agenda for the Board of Governors, and chairs the Board meetings. The current (2002) Chairman is Alan Greenspan

5. The most important policy-making body within the Fed is the Federal Open Market Committee (FOMC). All seven Board of Governors members are also on the FOMC. The president of the New York Federal Reserve Bank is always on the FOMC and the eleven other Reserve Bank presidents rotate through the remaining four seats on the FOMC. The FOMC buys or sells government securities (mostly T-bills) from or to major government securities dealers, who are, for the most part, major commercial banks. When the Fed buys T-bills, the banking system receives money from the Fed, increasing the money supply. When the Fed sells T-bills, the money supply decreases. As most of the government securities dealers are located in New York, the FOMC trading desk is located in the New York Federal Reserve Bank.

6. The FOMC meets eight times a year to revise monetary policy. They sometimes conduct telephone conference calls between meetings. Policy changes, including directions given to the trading desk and the Fed's judgment about the economic outlook, are announced immediately after a meeting. Minutes of FOMC meetings are released immediately after the subsequent meeting.

7. The Fed also serves as a "lender of last resort." Member banks may borrow from the Fed through the discount window. Banks that borrow too much or too often from the discount window in effect tell the Fed that they are experiencing stress. The Fed will then monitor these distressed banks very closely. Banks can avoid this uncomfortable increased scrutiny by keeping their use of the discount window limited.

8. The degree of independence the Fed enjoys from Congress and the President and the secrecy, the "mystique," surrounding much of the Fed's actions and decision-making processes is an area of ongoing controversy. Should the Fed be forced to provide greater disclosure of its deliberations? Does Congress really want to take responsibility for monetary policy, or are they actually happy to have the Fed serve as their "scapegoat?" Is the Fed really all that independent? As one observer put it, "the Fed watches the election results." That is, the Fed does respond to changes in the political climate in Washington.

TRUE/FALSE QUESTIONS

T F 1. For a period of time, from 1836 until the Civil War era, the United States did not have a central bank and notes issued by private banks, not the Federal government, were used as currency.

T F 2. The Board of Governors of the Federal Reserve System has seven members who are elected every two years in national elections.

T F 3. There are twelve districts in the Federal Reserve System and each district has its own Reserve Bank. However, all twelve of the Reserve Banks have their headquarters in Washington, D.C.

T F 4. The FOMC meets each day in the conference room of the New York Federal Reserve Bank.

T F 5. All seven members of the Board of Governors of the Federal Reserve System also serve on the FOMC.

T F 6. The FOMC, under the guidance of the Board of Governors of the Federal Reserve System, carries out United States monetary policy by buying and selling, in the open market, Treasury bills from and to the major securities dealers of New York City.

T F 7. The president of the New York Federal Reserve Bank usually chairs the FOMC.

T F 8. In addition to the president of the New York Federal Reserve Bank, the presidents of the Chicago and the San Francisco Reserve Banks also serve as permanent members of the FOMC.

Chapter 4 — The Federal Reserve System

T F 9. Given the sensitive nature of the banking information that the Fed possesses, it is no surprise that the Federal Reserve Board of Governors simply refuses to release minutes of its meetings.

T F 10. The twelve district Federal Reserve Banks operate clearinghouses that clear (i.e., move funds from the bank the on which check was written to the bank where the check was deposited) millions of dollars worth of checks each day.

T F 11. The U.S. Treasury's "transactions account," is maintained by the Fed and is, in effect, the federal government's checking account.

T F 12. The U.S. Treasury transactions account is excluded from M1 and therefore, by definition, is not money.

T F 13. When the FOMC purchases government securities on the open market, holding all other factors constant, the money supply increases.

T F 14. Under normal circumstances, commercial banks that are members of the Federal Reserve System can continuously fund their short-term requirements for reserves by borrowing at the Fed's "discount window."

T F 15. To be the "lender of last resort" means that the Fed is the last place a commercial bank suffering severe distress (such as a run on its deposits) would go to seek a loan.

T F 16. Monetary policies that are in the best long-term interest of the nation are often unpopular in the short-term.

T F 17. If the Federal Reserve were made more accountable to Congress, the President, and, ultimately, to the citizens of the United States, the actions of the Fed would be less likely to be influenced by short-tem election cycle pressures.

T F 18. Reserve requirements are set by the FOMC.

T F 19. The current required reserve ratio on time and savings deposits is 10%.

T F 20. The "fed funds" rate is the rate the Fed charges depository institutions that borrow reserves directly from the Fed.

T F 21. In general, banks that wish to create new branches or that wish to merge with or acquire other banks must seek approval from the Federal Reserve.

T F 22. Most observers agree that the Federal Open Market Committee wields great power over the U.S. financial markets. However, it remains a point of contention among analysts as to whether the power wielded by the Thrift Institutions Advisory Council does or does not exceed that of the FOMC.

T F 23. The westernmost district of the Federal Reserve System includes California and eight other states and the district's Federal Reserve Bank is located in Los Angeles.

T F   24. Five of the twelve members of the FOMC are directly appointed to the FOMC by the President of the United States with the advice and consent of the U.S. Senate.

T F   25. All commercial banks, whether they are federally chartered or state chartered, must join the Federal Reserve System.

MULTIPLE CHOICE QUESTIONS

1. The Federal Reserve could use which of the following tools to carry out monetary policy:
   a. changes in the discount rate
   b. changes in the required reserve ratio
   c. open market purchases and sales of government securities
   d. all of the above
   e. none of the above

2. After each of its meetings, the FOMC announces its assessment of the risks faced by the economy. Which of the following risks are specifically addressed in the announcement?
   a. corporate bond default risk and inflation risk
   b. inflation risk and liquidity risk
   c. excessive speculation and reserve requirement risk
   d. economic weakness and inflation risk

3. The Federal Reserve performs all of the following functions except:
   a. acts as lender of last resort
   b. forms the budget of the United States federal government
   c. implements U.S. monetary policy
   d. sets the required reserve ratios for the U.S banking system

4. All of the following are members of the FOMC except:
   a. the President of the New York Federal Reserve bank
   b. the President of the United States
   c. the Chair of the Board of Governors of the Federal Reserve System
   d. the members of the Board of Governors of the Federal Reserve System

5. The Federal Reserve's regulatory functions include monitoring compliance with which of the following laws:
   a. the Alien and Sedition Act
   b. the Fair Credit Billing Act
   c. the Interest Rate Reduction Act
   d. the Coinage Act

6. The Federal Reserve performs all the following functions except:
   a. provides a clearinghouse to clear checks
   b. maintains the U.S. Treasury's transactions account
   c. monitors compliance with the Community Reinvestment Act

d. establishes the price at which dollars can be exchanged for gold

7. All of the following cities are Federal Reserve Bank cities except:
    a. Los Angeles
    b. New York
    c. Richmond
    d. Cleveland

8. The FOMC trading desk is located in which Federal Reserve Bank?
    a. Los Angeles
    b. Chicago
    c. New York
    d. Philadelphia

9. Which of the following Federal Reserve actions would tend to reduce the money supply?
    a. open market purchases of government securities
    b. lowering the required reserve ratios
    c. increasing the discount rate
    d. all of the above
    e. none of the above

10. All of the following countries are members of the European Union except:
    a. the United Kingdom
    b. Sweden
    c. Portugal
    d. the United States

11. The Federal Reserve System is:
    a. exempt from many provisions of the Freedom of Information Act
    b. self-funded
    c. not obligated to obey the U.S. Constitution
    d. a and b
    e. all of the above

12. After each FOMC meeting:
    a. interest rates tend to rise
    b. interest rates tend to fall
    c. the FOMC releases the minutes of that meeting
    d. the FOMC provides an announcement as to its current policy stance

13. The Federal Reserve System was initially formed in response to:
    a. the Great Depression of the 1930s
    b. the banking panic of 1893
    c. the "Crime of 1873"
    d. the banking crisis of 1907

14. Which, if any, of the following statements are true?
    a. the Federal Reserve is independent of the U.S. Congress and, therefore, is not subject to obey laws passed by the Congress over a President's veto
    b. no action undertaken by the Federal Reserve is subject to review by the Supreme Court of the United States
    c. the Federal Reserve System has the power to appoint its own ambassadors to other nations and to the United Nations
    d. all of the above are true
    e. none of the above are true

15. Monetary policy has the primary objective(s):
    a. to ensure sufficient money and credit is available to allow the economy to expand along its long-term growth path
    b. to maintain long-term growth with little or no inflation
    c. to minimize short-term fluctuations around the long-term trend
    d. a and b
    e. all of the above

16. The Federal Reserve was created by:
    a. the Federal Reserve Act of 1913
    b. the Banking Reform Act of 1933
    c. the Banking Reform Act of 1935
    d. none of the above

FILL IN QUESTIONS

1. To lend money to commercial banks during emergencies is known as the _____ function.

2. The ruling body of the Federal Reserve System is the _____, which is located in Washington, D.C.

3. The largest and most important district Federal Reserve Bank is the Federal Reserve Bank of _____.

4. The _____ formulates monetary policy and oversees its implementation.

5. The Treasury's _____ account, maintained by the Federal Reserve System, is, in effect, the federal government's checking account.

6. In the view of the Fed, borrowing from the discount window is a _____, not a _____ and thus banks are encouraged to borrow from the discount window only when absolutely necessary.

7. The proportion of deposits that must be held in the form of reserve assets is set by the Fed and is known as the _____ _____ ratio.

8. The stimulus to create the Federal Reserve System was the banking crisis of _____, which was, in part, caused by the destruction of the banking system in the western United States due to the San Francisco earthquake of 1906.

9. In order to expand the money supply and reduce interest rates, the FOMC would _____ Treasury bills.

10. Blaming the Fed when things go wrong is an example of using the Fed as a convenient _____.

ESSAY QUESTIONS

1. The Federal Reserve System was designed with twelve districts to decentralize monetary authority and power. The framers of the 1913 act also had in mind that each district bank would be able to set its own discount rate. Indeed, in 1913 the framers of the act thought business conditions to be so varied by region that each Fed district would have its own set of interest rates altogether. Discuss why this never happened (or, at least, never happened to any great extent). Why do U.S. interest rates generally reflect national economic conditions, instead of local or regional economic conditions? When the FOMC buys or sells T-bills in New York, why do interest rates in Dubuque and Little Rock and other U.S. cities change?

2. Write a short essay either supporting or attacking the following debate topic. Resolved: the Chair of the Federal Reserve Board of Governors should be elected to a four year term by the citizens of the Republic in national elections held during non-Presidential election years.

3. The text points out that "sweep accounts" reduce the effectiveness of changing reserve requirements in conducting monetary policy. List two or three other financial innovations that might also reduce the effectiveness of Federal Reserve actions.

INTERNET EXERCISES

1. A Federal Reserve Bank of Minneapolis Web site - http://woodrow.mpls.frb.fed.us/info/policy - provides a nice description of the goals of monetary policy and the tools available to achieve these goals. Of particular note is the link to the FOMC. Take a look.

2. Conspiracy buffs will have their arguments rebutted (although their paranoia might make it difficult for them to realize it) if they visit Dr. Edward Flaherty's site at http://members.home.net/flaherty15/conspire.htm#2. I intended to also provide you with the

Web address of people that believe in these conspiracies, but I'm hesitant to take seriously anyone who uses the word "imbezzlement" on their site and can't be bothered to use a spell checker to change it to embezzlement.

3. Some folks, and I am one of those folks, say that the best way to know if the Chair of the Board of Governors is doing a good job is to see if everybody is complaining. If Democrats are unhappy, but Republicans are also unhappy, if management is unhappy, but labor is also unhappy, etc., then the Fed Chair is doing his or her job well. Use a search engine such as Yahoo or Excite to search for "Federal Reserve." Then click on the "News" or "Current Events" link. Who's unhappy with the Chair of the Board of Governors this week?

5

Interest Rates and Bond Prices

SUMMARY

1. A dollar received today is of greater value than a dollar to be received in the future because we can invest today's dollar and earn a return on our investment. We could place today's dollar into a bank account that pays 6% interest, for example. In one year, we would be able to withdraw $1.06 from our account for each dollar we deposit today. That is, $100 today is equivalent to $106 one year from today, if the appropriate interest rate over that one-year period is 6%. Thus, the future value of $100 one year from now at 6% is $106 ($100 times 1.06 equals $106). Finding such future values is called compounding.

2. Interest rates allow us to calculate the equivalent values of dollars that exist at differing points in time. To continue our example, if the one-year rate is 6%, $1.00 to be received in one year would be equivalent to $0.94340 today. We can find this result by dividing $1.00 by 1.06. As a check on the accuracy of this calculation we can also see that if you increase $0.94340 by 6% (by multiplying $0.94340 by 1.06), the result is $1.00. We say that the present value of $1.00 to be received in one year at 6% interest is $0.94340. Finding such present values is called discounting. Note that discounting (*dividing* by one plus the interest rate) is merely the inverse of compounding (*multiplying* by one plus the interest rate).

3. Compound interest means that one earns interest on both the initial principal and also on the interest as that interest accrues (is added to) the principal. Again let us suppose that the correct interest rate is 6% only now we will let our savings accumulate for three years. Starting with an initial deposit of $100, after one year we have $106. In the second year we will add 6% to this $106 (i.e., multiply $106 by 1.06) so that the value at the end of the second year is $112.36. In the third year, add 6% to the $112.36 ($112.36 * 1.06) and we see that the FV of 100 in three years at 6% compounded annually is $119.1016.

4. In general, then, one uses the following formula (formula (5-4) in the text) to find future values

$$V_n = V_0(1 + i)^n$$

Chapter 5   Interest Rates and Bond Prices

One uses the inverse of (5-4), given below, to find present values (the present value formula is formula (5-5) in the text)

$$V_0 = V_n / (1 + i)^n$$

In each formula, V_n is the future value at time n, V_0 is the present value, i is the appropriate interest rate, and n is the number of years.

5. Changes in interest rates impact all financial assets, but they are especially important in pricing bonds. The price of a bond is the present value of the stream of payments the bond issuer promises to pay. The stream of payments consists of periodic payments (called coupons) and a final payment when the bond matures (known as the face value, the par value, the maturity value, as well as several more synonyms). The dollars of coupon paid each year equals the coupon rate times the par value. Thus, a bond with a face value of $1,000 and a coupon rate of 7.5% would pay a coupon of $75 per year until maturity. At maturity, the bond would pay $1,075 (par value plus the last coupon).

6. To price a bond, apply (5-5) to each of the coupon payments and to the maturity payment and sum these present values. If interest rates go up, the prices of existing bonds go down (except for adjustable rate bonds whose coupons are adjusted to match the higher interest rate, see Chapter 10). If interest rates fall, bond prices rise, although the call feature of some bonds might mean they don't increase very much in price as interest rates fall (see Chapter 10). Bond prices that have risen above the bond's maturity value are said to trade at a premium. Conversely, discount bonds trade below par value.

7. Since interest rates are so important in determining the prices of bonds, we should make an effort to understand those factors that determine interest rates. We start by noting that the set of interest rates represents the price of money lent out for various lengths of time. Then like all good economists, we note that prices are determined by supply and demand; in the case of interest rates, the supply of and demand for loanable funds. Then we look at those things that might cause the supply of loanable funds or the demand for loanable funds to change. Three important factors appear: changes in GDP, Federal Reserve actions that change the money supply, and expected inflation.

8. Interest rates tend to increase when the economy grows more rapidly. Thus, interest rates have a cyclical quality to them. When the economy is becoming stronger, interest rates tend to rise as businesses borrow to finance expansions. When the economy weakens, rates tend to fall as businesses stop expanding. Interest rates tend to fall when the Federal Reserve increases the money supply. Finally, interest rates increase when people expect inflation to be higher. Using the mathematical notation for a function, the text writes:

$$i = f(Y^+, M^-, p^{+e})$$

where i represents interest rates, f(•) reads "is/are a function of," Y^+ represents GDP with the plus sign indicating the interest rate and GDP relationship is positive, M^- is the money supply with the minus sign meaning that the relationship between interest rates and money supply is negative (more money causes interest rates to fall), and p^{+e} represents the positive relationship between interest rates and expected inflation.

9. Inflation is typically measured as the percentage change in either the Consumer Price Index (CPI) or the Producer Price Index (PPI). The CPI is appropriate for changes in the cost of goods and services purchased by a typical consumer. The PPI gives a better indication of changes in the cost of doing business. Both indices are calculated as the prices of a basket of goods at one time divided by the prices of that same basket of goods in the previous period. The inflation rate is the percentage change in these ratios. The real rate of return is approximately equal to the nominal interest rate minus the expected rate of inflation.

10. The first appendix to this chapter describes a particular type of bond that has an infinite coupon stream and no maturity date known as a "consol." The present value of a consol is found by dividing the coupon by the interest rate. The second appendix compares the supply and demand for money model of Chapter 2 to the supply and demand for loanable funds model of Chapter 5.

TRUE/FALSE QUESTIONS

T F 1. Holding all other factors constant, if the rate of growth in the economy slows, the demand for money will fall and interest rates will rise.

T F 2. Calculating the present value of a given future value at an appropriate interest rate is called discounting.

T F 3. When interest rates increase, present values decline.

T F 4. If a bond's coupon rate and the appropriate rate for discounting the bond's cash flows happen by odd circumstance to be equal, the bond will sell at par.

T F 5. A bond whose par value exceeds its current price is said to be selling at a premium.

T F 6. The value of a dollar to be received today exceeds the value of a dollar to be received sometime in the future.

T F 7. Compounding is the inverse operation to discounting.

T F 8. If the Federal Reserve takes actions to increase the money supply, interest rates are more likely to rise than to fall.

T F 9. The supply of loanable funds would fall if the national savings rate were to increase.

T F 10. In an attempt to bring the nation out of a recession, or to head off a looming recession, the Federal Reserve would attempt to increase the rate of return on domestic savings.

T F 11. In order to earn compound interest on a financial asset, any interest actually paid out in cash to an investor must be reinvested into the same or similar financial asset.

T F 12. If interest rates rise, holding all other factors constant, the supply of loanable funds will also rise.

T F 13. Businesses are more likely to expand when interest rates are relatively low, holding all else constant.

T F 14. If people expect prices to generally increase, it will take higher interest rates to encourage them to forego current consumption and increase their savings.

T F 15. Periodic payments made to bondholders are known as coupon payments.

T F 16. An example of money illusion would be when an investor believes himself to be better off because he received a 2% higher interest rate on his savings account this year compared to last year. However, expected inflation this year is three percentage points higher than last year.

T F 17. If expected inflation is 4% and the nominal interest rate is 3%, the real rate of return is negative.

T F 18. To reduce the fear of expected inflation, the Federal Reserve would increase the money supply.

T F 19. The current price of a bond is equal to the sum of the future values of the bond's cash flows compounded at the appropriate interest rate.

T F 20. If the appropriate interest rate was 8%, a consol with a coupon of $2.40 per year would sell for $30.00.

T F 21. If the appropriate interest rate was 8%, a bond with a coupon rate of 6% would sell at a discount.

T F 22. A zero coupon bond (that is, a bond with a coupon rate of zero percent) would have no value.

T F 23. The equilibrium interest rate is that interest rate at which the supply of loanable funds and the demand for loanable funds are equal.

T F 24. An increase in the productivity of capital investment would tend to increase interest rates.

MULTIPLE CHOICE QUESTIONS

1. If interest rates increase:
    a. present values fall
    b. people are less likely to save
    c. future values fall
    d. businesses are more likely to borrow

2. If the supply of loanable funds increases and the demand for loanable funds decreases:
   a. the effect on interest rates is indeterminate
   b. interest rates will rise
   c. interest rates will fall
   d. none of the above

3. You place $1,000 into a mutual fund that earns 12% interest per year. Forty years later you withdraw the funds to pay for your granddaughter's college education. How much is in the account when you make the withdrawal?
   a. $93,051
   b. $56,694
   c. $44,800
   d. none of the above within $2,000

4. If the nominal interest rate is 7.00% and expected inflation is 2.00%, the real rate of return is approximately:
   a. 1.40%
   b. 5.00%
   c. 9.00%
   d. 7.00%

5. Find the present value of $2,500 to be received in five years if the appropriate interest rate is 7%.
   a. $5,630
   b. $2,493
   c. $2,325
   d. $1,782

6. If the price of the basket of goods and services used in calculating the CPI moves from $725 in period one to $857 in period two, and assuming the base period cost of the basket was $500, the CPI in period one is:
   a. 725.00
   b. 145.00
   c. 118.21
   d. none of the above

7. If the price of the basket of goods and services used in calculating the CPI moves from $725 in period one to $857 in period two, and assuming the base period cost of the basket was $500, the CPI in period two is:
   a. 857.00
   b. 171.40
   c. 145.00
   d. none of the above

8. If the price of the basket of goods and services used in calculating the CPI moves from $725 in period one to $857 in period two, and assuming the base period cost of the basket was $500, the rate of inflation from period one to period two is:
   a. 0.15%
   b. 1.18%
   c. 18.21%
   d. none of the above

Chapter 5   Interest Rates and Bond Prices

9. If interest rates fall, the prices of existing fixed-coupon bonds will:
   a. increase
   b. decrease
   c. remain the same
   d. continue to be unpredictable

10. A consol with a coupon of $7.25 currently is priced at $145. What is the appropriate rate of return used in pricing this consol?
    a. 10%
    b. 8%
    c. 5%
    d. 2%

11. How much would you be willing to pay to acquire a zero coupon consol?
    a. nothing, such a bond would be worthless
    b. it depends on the appropriate rate of interest for the bond
    c. it depends on the value of coupon paying consols of equivalent maturity
    d. it depends on my marginal tax rate

12. A bond that pays an annual coupon equal to 6% of par value, that has a par value of $1,000, and has three years left to maturity, would have a present value of $948.46 if the appropriate interest rate used to discount the bond's cash flows is:
    a. 12%
    b. 10%
    c. 8%
    d. 6%

13. A bond currently selling for $1,106.38 has a face value of $1,000, four years left to maturity, an appropriate discount rate of 5%, and pays it coupons annually. What is the bond's coupon rate?
    a. 4%
    b. 5%
    c. 6%
    d. 8%
    e. 10%

14. A zero coupon bond with eight years to maturity and an appropriate discount rate of 7% would sell for:
    a. $1,070
    b. $ 582
    c. $ 560
    d. none of the above within $50

15. Price a bond that has six years to maturity, a par value of $1,000, a coupon rate of 5% with coupons paid annually, and that has an appropriate discount rate of 5%
    a. $1,000
    b. $ 958
    c. $ 675
    d. $ 556

16. Assume that two bonds have equal appropriate discount rates. One bond is a zero coupon bond with seven years to maturity and a present value of $710.68. The second bond has four years to maturity and pays an annual coupon equal to 7% of its $1,000 par value. What is the present value of the second bond?
    a. $1,225.46
    b. $1,070.92
    c. $1,000.00
    d. $ 710.68

17. Which of the following bonds has the highest appropriate discount rate?
    a. a three year bond with a coupon rate of 4%, coupons paid annually, a par value of $1,000, and a present value of $972.77
    b. a ten year zero coupon bond with a face value of $1,000 that is currently priced at $558.39
    c. a two year bond with a coupon rate of 8%, coupons paid annually, a par value of $1,000, and a present value of $1,075.44
    d. a five year zero coupon bond with a face value of $1,000 and a current price of $783.53

18. A bond with one year to maturity, a 5% coupon rate, coupons paid annually, and a par value of $1,000 currently trades at a price of $972.22. If expected inflation is 4%, the real return on this bond is approximately:
    a. 8%
    b. 6%
    c. 4%
    d. 0%

19. An investor borrows money from a bank at a fixed interest rate. If actual inflation over the period of the loan exceeds the rate of inflation that was expected at the time the loan was made:
    a. the borrower will be happier about the higher inflation than will the lender
    b. the lender will be happier about the higher inflation than will the borrower
    c. neither the borrower nor the lender will care as the rate was fixed at the time the loan was entered into
    d. the premise of this question is faulty as actual inflation can never exceed expected inflation

20. If demand for loanable funds rises while the supply of loanable funds also rises:
    a. interest rates will rise
    b. interest rates will fall
    c. the effect on interest rates is indeterminate
    d. the economy is in recession

FILL IN QUESTIONS

1. Bonds pay two kinds of cash flows – a recurring stream of payments known as _____, and an ending payment known as the _____.

2. Future values are calculated by _____ a given present value by $(1 + i)^n$.

3. Present values are calculated by _____ a given future value by $(1 + i)^n$.

4. The most typical face value for a bond is _____.

5. When a bond sells at par, the coupon rate of the bond equals _____.

6. If the appropriate discount rate to use in discounting a bond's cash flows exceeds that bond's coupon rate, the bond will sell at a _____.

7. The demand for loanable funds typically increases when GDP _____.

8. If expected inflation falls, but the nominal rate remains the same, the real rate has _____.

9. A bond that promises to pay a fixed coupon in perpetuity (i.e., forever) is called a _____.

10. As the national economy begins to expand from the trough of a recession, interest rates are likely to _____.

ESSAY QUESTIONS

1. Refer to the demand for money vs. the supply of money model given in Chapter 2. Recall that in that model the supply of money was depicted as a vertical line (i.e., a slope of infinity). However, the demand for loanable funds vs. the supply of loanable funds model presented in this chapter depicts the supply of loanable funds as a sloped line (with a slope of something less than infinity). Explain why the supply of money at a given point in time is fixed as interest rates change, holding all else constant, but the supply of loanable funds will increase as interest rates increase (and vice-versa). (Hint: refer to Appendix 5-B).

2. Suppose that over the next five years I want to accumulate $10,000 as a down payment on a house. If I can save money in a savings account that pays 5% per year, how much would I need to deposit today, in one lump sum, to reach my savings goal? Now try to find how much I would need to save in five equal payments, each made one year from today, to reach my goal. (Hint: find, in turn, the present value of $1 one year away, of $1 two years away, of $1 three years away, of $1 four years away, and of $1 five years away. Add these five present values. Divide the present value of $10,000 five years away by the sum of the $1 present value factors.)

3. Interest rates tend to rise when the economy is strengthening and fall when the economy is growing weaker. However, the risk of default on corporate bonds might also grow as the economy weakens. If both of these statements are true, which bond prices will tend to move more as the economy weakens – corporate bonds or default free government bonds?

INTERNET EXERCISES

1. Dr. Tim Mayes of the Metropolitan State College of Denver has a useful Web site on using financial calculators. Calculators make it much easier to do the time value of money problems of this and later chapters. Take a look by going to http://clem.mscd.edu/~mayest/calculators/calculator_tutorials_index.

2. A short history lesson might reinforce the idea of who wins and who loses when actual inflation over the period of a loan is higher than or lower than the expected inflation at the time the interest rate on the loan was fixed. William Jennings Bryan ran for President of the United States in 1896 espousing the free (i.e., unlimited) conversion of silver into U.S. coins. The opponents of Bryan wanted the nation to continue to allow only gold coins to be used for money, as was established in the Coinage Act of 1873. Many of Bryan's supporters were farmers or silver mine owners or workers. It seems fairly obvious that silver mine owners would like a ready outlet and a constant dollar price for the silver they produce. But why would farmers and other laborers back "free coinage of silver?" Francois Micheloud presents an entertaining discussion of this period of American history at his Web site http://www.micheloud.com/FXM/MH/index.htm.

6

The Structure of Interest Rates

SUMMARY

1. Many interest rates, not just a single interest rate, exist at any one time. One useful way to organize interest rates is by maturity of the instrument. Short-term rates often differ from long-term rates. The yield curve graphs the relationship between interest rates and their term to maturity.

2. The shape of the yield curve is of interest. If longer term-rates are higher than shorter-term interest rates, that fact has different economic implications than if the opposite condition holds. Three theories that attempt to explain the shape of the yield curve are presented in the text. Underlying all three theories are investors' expectations of changes in interest rates. The three theories are: the expectations theory, the liquidity premium theory, and the preferred habitat theory.

3. The expectations theory holds that investors' expectations about future short-term rates determine the shape of the yield curve. This theory postulates that the long-term rate is the geometric average of the one plus the current short-term rate and one plus the short-term rate expected in the future. For a simple two-period world, if the current one-period rate is 5% and the current two-period rate is 8%, then under the expectations theory, people, in the aggregate, expect the one-period rate one period into the future to be 11.086%. You can verify the 11.086% for the expected one-period rate one year into the future by finding the geometric average of (1 + .05) and (1 + .11086). To find a geometric average, multiply the items and then take the nth root of the product, where n is the number of items. In this case, multiply 1.05 times 1.110896 and take the second root (the square root). Thus, 1.05 * 1.110896 = 1.16640. The square root of 1.16640 is 1.08, which matches one plus the current two-year rate (1 + .08).

4. Interest rate expectations are a positively related to expected GDP growth, inversely related to expected growth in the money supply, and positively related to expected inflation. Under the expectations theory, a positively sloped yield curve indicates that investors expect short-term rates in the future will be higher than current short-term rates. Upward sloping yield curves are often observed near the trough of the business cycle. A downward sloping yield curve indicates that investors expect interest rates to fall. Downward sloping yield curves are often observed near the peak of the business cycle.

5. More often than not, the yield curve is upward sloping. Thus, there is apparently a bias in investors' expectations. The liquidity premium theory explains this bias. It argues that investors prefer short-term investments, all else held equal. Short-term investments are naturally more liquid – they will

Chapter 6   The Structure of Interest Rates

turn into cash sooner than long-term investments will. In order to "pull" investors into longer dated instruments, borrowers must pay a higher interest rate than would be true under pure expectations. This higher rate reflects a "premium" over the pure expectations interest rates.

6. The preferred habitat theory argues that investors have a preferred maturity, not always just the shortest maturity. To pull or push investors into a non-preferred maturity, whether it be a shorter maturity or a longer maturity, borrowers have to pay a higher interest rate than they would under pure expectations.

7. At least two other factors affect the structure of interest rates. They are credit risk and taxes. Bonds with a greater risk of default should pay higher interest. Bond ratings provided by rating agencies such as Moody's or Standard & Poor's attempt to measure the probability of default. Municipal bonds (bonds issued by state or local governments) often pay coupons that are exempt from federal taxation. This feature allows municipals to pay lower interest rates to investors. High tax bracket investors will be particularly attracted to municipals.

TRUE/FALSE QUESTIONS

T F   1. Holding all other factors constant, if investors revise their expectations regarding future interest rates upward, then current interest rates will fall.

T F   2. A corporate bond rated AAA by Standard & Poor's would most likely pay a higher interest rate than a similar maturity corporate bond rated BBB by Standard & Poor's.

T F   3. An investor in the 42% marginal tax bracket would prefer a municipal bond that pays 5% interest to a corporate bond that pays 9%.

T F   4. Current long-term interest rates are positively related to current short-term interest rates, expected short-term interest rates, and to the liquidity premium.

T F   5. If short-term rates are 6% and long-term rates are 5%, the yield curve is downward sloping and it suggests the possibility of a recession in the near future.

T F   6. The term structure of interest rates is the graphical representation of the yield curve.

T F   7. The current one-year rate is 4%. You happen to know that investors truly expect the one-year rate one year from now to be 5%. If the observed current two-year rate is 4.75%, these conditions are more supportive of the liquidity premium theory than the (pure or unbiased) expectations theory.

T F   8. To calculate the geometric average of a series of returns, subtract one from each return, multiply the resulting numbers, and take the nth root of the product.

T F   9. Holding all other factors constant, if investors expect strong economic growth in the near future interest rates are likely to fall.

T F 10. For the most part, in the years following World War II, yield curves have been upward sloping.

T F 11. If borrowers expect long-term rates to fall in the near future, they would prefer to issue short-term bonds now.

T F 12. Risk averse investors will never invest in risky investments even if the investment offers very high potential returns.

T F 13. If the risk premium is sufficient, in the opinion of the investor, to compensate for the risk taken, a risk averse investor would invest in a risky investment, even a very risky investment.

T F 14. If the federal government lowers tax rates across the board, municipal bonds will most likely be forced to increase the interest they pay in order to remain competitive with corporate bonds.

T F 15. Using the Standard & Poor's ratings, the highest quality bonds (least likely to default) are those rated AAAA.

T F 16. One-year rates are 5.5%. Two-year rates are 6%. Under the expectations theory, the expected one-year rate one year from now is 11.83%.

T F 17. Assume that the liquidity premium theory best explains the shape of the yield curve. If so, the yield curve could never be downward sloping, even if investors expect future short-term rates to drop dramatically.

T F 18. There is no need to rate securities issued by state and local governments as such bonds can never default.

T F 19. If corporate bonds offer a return of 9% and equivalent risk tax-exempt municipals offer a return of 6%, investors in the 20% marginal tax bracket will prefer the corporate bonds.

T F 20. The higher the marginal tax bracket, the higher the interest rate corporate bonds need to offer to attract investors, all other factors held constant.

MULTIPLE CHOICE QUESTIONS

1. One-year rates are 4.75%. Two-year rates are 4.5% Under the (pure or unbiased) expectations theory, the one-year rate one year from now is expected to be:
   a. 5.00%
   b. 4.25%
   c. 4.00%
   d. 3.75%

2. If the marginal tax bracket is 35%, which of the following statements is not true:
   a. an investor would prefer a municipal bond with a 5.50% return to a corporate bond with a 9.20% return
   b. an investor would prefer a municipal bond with a 5.00% return to a corporate bond with a 7.25% return
   c. an investor would prefer a municipal bond with a 7.00% return to a corporate bond with a 10.25% return
   d. an investor would prefer a municipal bond with a 6.50% return to a corporate bond with a 9.20% return

3. If marginal tax rates are reduced but interest rates remain steady (possibly because expected inflation increased or the money supply is expected to be reduced), and holding all else constant:
   a. corporate bond prices will fall
   b. municipal bond prices will fall
   c. municipal bond prices will rise
   d. both municipal and corporate bond prices will remain the same

4. As the business cycle enters an expansion stage:
   a. interest rates will typically be low and rising
   b. interest rates will typically be low and still falling
   c. interest rates will typically be high and still rising
   d. interest rates will typically be high but beginning to fall

5. All of the following are theories that attempt to explain the shape of the yield curve except:
   a. the yield curve theory
   b. the expectations theory
   c. segmented markets
   d. preferred habitat

6. Bonds that have greater credit risk:
   a. would be rated B or BB or BBB rather than A or AA or AAA
   b. would generally offer higher rates of return to investors
   c. have a greater chance of defaulting
   d. all of the above

7. The state of Nevada has no state income tax (as of this writing). Suppose an investor from Nevada is considering the purchase of a tax-exempt bond issued by a New York state housing agency. The Nevada investor is in the 28% federal tax bracket. A New York investor, also in the 28% federal tax bracket is considering purchasing the same bond. She, however, also pays New York state tax at a marginal rate of 6%. Assuming the bond is exempt from both New York and federal taxes and holding all other factors equal:
   a. the Nevada investor will be willing to pay a higher price to acquire the bond than the New York investor will be willing to pay
   b. the New York investor will be willing to pay a higher price to acquire the bond than the Nevada investor will be willing to pay
   c. both investors will be willing to pay the same price for the bond
   d. the bond will not be available for sale outside the state of New York

Chapter 6   The Structure of Interest Rates

8. The liquidity premium is defined as:
   a. the extra return required to induce borrowers to borrow long-term rather than short-term
   b. the difference between the returns on SEC registered bonds and those bonds that are exempt from registration with the SEC
   c. the expectation that future short-term rates will be lower than current short-term rates
   d. the extra return required to induce lenders to lend long-term rather than short-term

9. Which of the following presents in the correct order bonds arranged from shortest maturity to longest maturity.
   a. Treasury bonds, Treasury bills, consols
   b. consols, Treasury bills, Treasury bonds
   c. Treasury bills, Treasury bonds, consols
   d. none of the above

10. Holding all other factors constant, as interest rates rise:
    a. borrowers are more likely to borrow
    b. lenders are more likely to lend
    c. lenders are less likely to lend
    d. existing bond prices will rise

11. Progressive tax rates (holding all other factor constant):
    a. make it easier to sell municipal (tax exempt) bonds
    b. force interest rates on tax exempt securities to be higher than they would otherwise be
    c. increase the after tax rate of return on tax exempt bonds
    d. a and c

12. Find the geometric average of the following series of returns: 4% in the first year, 6% in the second year, -3% (negative three percent) in the third year.
    a. 6.12%
    b. 4.33%
    c. 2.33%
    d. 2.26%

13. A one-year zero coupon bond with a par value of $1,000 is currently priced at $952.38. A two-year zero coupon bond is currently selling for $890.00. Calculate the expected one-year rate one year from today.
    a. 5.45%
    b. 5.98%
    c. 7.01%
    d. 8.00%

14. If the one-year rate is 6% and the expected one-year rate one year from today is 6%, today's two year rate must be:
    a. 6%
    b. between 5% and 6%
    c. less than 5%
    d. greater than 6%

15. If inflation is expected to be lower in the near future than in the recent past, long-term rates are likely to:
    a. rise
    b. remain the same
    c. fall
    d. more information is needed before one can make this determination

16. A zero coupon bond with one year to maturity and a par value of $1,000 is selling today for $892.86. The expected one-year rate one year from now is 10%. Calculate today's price of a two-year zero coupon bond with a par value of $1,000.
    a. $1,000.00
    b. $ 998.92
    c. $ 976.43
    d. $ 811.62

17. Assume that over the past week the prices of most long-term corporate bonds have fallen. Which of the following explanations is most consistent with that observation?
    a. the Federal Reserve has loosened monetary policy
    b. expectations of inflation have increased
    c. new GDP estimates show the economy slowing, but not slowing sufficiently to endanger corporate debt servicing
    d. default risk is generally believed to be decreasing

18. Which of the following strategies is most attractive to an investor with a two-year time horizon? Round your answers to five decimal places.
    a. purchase a one-year bond with a return of 5% followed by a one-year bond that is expected to return 5.5%
    b. purchase a two-year bond that offers a return of 5.25%
    c. a and b provide equivalent wealth at time two; therefore, the investor is indifferent to this choice
    d. change his time horizon to one year.

19. A taxpayer whose marginal federal tax rate is less than the average marginal federal tax rate is:
    a. likely to be more attracted to corporate bonds than to municipal bonds
    b. likely to be less attracted to corporate bonds than to municipal bonds
    c. likely to be a high-income earner
    d. likely to pay more in state taxes than those in the same state who have an above average marginal federal tax rate

FILL IN QUESTIONS

1. The graphical depiction of the term structure of interest rates is known as the _____.

2. Under the (pure or unbiased) expectations theory of the term structure of interest rates, observed interest rates are based on the _____ average of current short-term rates and expected short-term rates.

3. If interest rates are expected to rise in the near future, lenders will be _____ willing to lend short-term.

4. If expected inflation is high, but not very variable, interest rates will also be high and interest rates will have _____ volatility.

5. Both the preferred habitat and the _____ theories of the term structure of interest rates postulate, to a greater or lesser degree, that the prices of short-term instruments and the prices of long-term instruments are determined by supply and demand in their separate markets.

6. The yield curve most often slopes _____.

7. The two most widely known credit rating agencies are _____ and _____.

8. When a bond sells at par, the coupon rate of the bond equals _____.

9. The risk premium on federal government (Treasury) bonds is _____.

10. The most widely accepted explanation for the shape of the yield curve is the _____ theory.

ESSAY QUESTIONS

1. Many state and local bonds pay coupons that are exempt from state and local income taxes of those same states as well as federal income taxes. Thus, California bonds might be exempt from California income tax as well as federal income tax, and New York bonds exempt from New York income tax, etc. Many of the states with the highest state income tax rates (New York, California, Pennsylvania, among others) also issue the greatest number of tax-exempt bonds. Progressive tax rates, where higher income earners are taxed at higher marginal rates, are designed to redistribute income from high income earners to low income earners. But the very states with the high state tax rates issue bonds that allow high-income earners to avoid the payment of tax. Why? (Hint: there's certainly no easy answer to this question and there may be no answer at all. I am asking you to form an informed opinion on the matter).

2. Bonds rated Baa (by Moody's) or BBB (by Standard & Poor's) and higher are referred to as investment grade bonds. They have little speculative risk. What pejorative (i.e., not very nice) name is given to bonds rated at or below Ba or BB? (Hint: search for "Michael Milken" on the Internet.)

3. One can observe, on occasion, upward sloping yield curves that were not followed by periods of rising interest rates. One can also observe downward sloping yield curves that were not followed by falling interest rates. What does this say about expectations?

INTERNET EXERCISES

1. Go to Moody's Investors Services Web page - http://www.moodys.com. Click on the link labeled "Watchlist." Select North America from the menu that pops up. Are more North American bonds being considered for a possible downgrade or are more being considered for an upgrade? Is there a bias at work here? Will investors care more about Moody's or S&P missing downgrading a bond that deserved to be downgraded (i.e., it defaults) or will they be more interested in knowing if the agencies correctly rate high quality debt?

2. Bloomberg is one of the largest providers of financial data in the world. Go to http://www.bloomberg.com. Select "U.S. Treasuries" under the "Markets" menu and take a look at the current yield curve. Does it look like interest rates are expected to rise or to fall? Has the yield curve changed very much over the previous day?

7

Market Efficiency

SUMMARY

1. As described under the expectations theory of the term structure of interest rates (see Chapter 6), long-term rates are determined by current and expected short-term rates. Short-term rates and expected short-term rates are themselves determined by current and expected national income, the current and expected supply of money, and expected inflation. Prices of existing financial instruments respond to interest rate changes. When interest rates go up, the prices of most existing financial instruments go down. When interest rates go down, prices go up. Stock prices also reflect expected earnings. When earnings are expected to increase, stock prices rise. When earnings are expected to fall, stock prices fall.

2. In equilibrium, financial assets that have equivalent risk, including liquidity risk, will also have equivalent returns. Investors and borrowers form opinions regarding risk, liquidity, and return and choose assets that have, for them, the most attractive combination. SSUs and DSUs form these opinions using "adaptive expectations" and "rational expectations." Adaptive expectations essentially argues that people form opinions based on past events, especially the more recent past events. Rational expectations argues that opinions are the best guesses possible given all available information.

3. If in the process of forming these opinions and acting (trading) based on these opinions, SSUs and DSUs set supply and demand conditions such that the prices of financial assets are correct, we say the market is efficient. By "correct" we generally mean that the prices truly reflect the information available at the time the prices are set. Changes in the available information set, then, will cause the prices of financial assets to change. The speed and accuracy of these adjustments also casts evidence on the efficiency of the market. In an efficient market, prices will adjust to information set changes quickly and accurately on average.

4. If markets are efficient, one cannot earn above average returns, over the long run, unless one accepts above average risk. Another way of stating this is to say that if the market is efficient, then after properly adjusting for risk, including liquidity risk, all assets pay the same risk-adjusted return. Speculative bubbles and other evidence of market overreaction, such as becoming either too optimistic or too pessimistic, cast doubt on the efficiency of the market. However, in well-developed, liquid markets such as those of the United States, Western Europe and Japan, markets appear to be relatively efficient. It is difficult to find investors who have been able to earn consistent, long-term, risk-adjusted, excess returns in these markets.

5. Flow-of-funds analysis helps investors analyze information relative to the formation of expectations of GDP growth, money supply changes, inflation, and changes in interest rates. Dividing the economy into sectors – the typical structure being households, non-financial businesses, government, financial intermediaries, and non-U.S. entities – and calculating how funds flow across these sectors gives clues as to whether the supply of loanable funds and/or the demand for loanable funds will change. When a sector changes from surplus to deficit, or when a sector goes more into surplus or more into deficit, other sectors must show offsetting changes. Surplus and deficits across all sectors, in total, must be equal. These flow-of-funds can increase or decrease supply of or demand for loanable funds. Supply and demand conditions for loanable funds, of course, determine interest rates and vice-versa.

TRUE/FALSE QUESTIONS

T F 1. The key determinants of long-term interest rates are investors' past experiences, rather than their expectations regarding future events..

T F 2. If financial markets are efficient, then it is impossible to earn positive returns on investments.

T F 3. If financial markets are efficient, than all readily available information is reflected in the prices of securities.

T F 4. Efficient markets respond quickly and accurately to changes in relevant information.

T F 5. If markets are efficient, one can earn above average returns, but only by accepting above average risk.

T F 6. If people form their opinions based solely on adaptive expectations, than assessments of future events will not be reflected in those opinions.

T F 7. If financial markets are efficient, investors will gain little or nothing from the study of past prices and past volumes of securities' trading as these past events are already reflected into prices.

T F 8. Both rational expectations and adaptive expectations reference past events; however, adaptive expectations theory argues that people also adapt their opinions to their assessments of the likelihood of future outcomes.

T F 9. If financial markets are efficient, investors will gain little or nothing from the study of publicly available information such as a company's balance sheet or income statement as this public information is already reflected in securities' prices.

T F 10. If financial markets are efficient, investors will gain little or nothing from trades based on "insider information" as this information is already reflected in securities' prices.

T F 11. The "greater fool" theory suggests that an investor might knowingly pay more for a security than it is truly worth (which seems like a foolish thing to do) because an even more foolish investor will pay an even higher price to buy the security in the future.

T F 12. In order for a market to be efficient, all participants in the market need to have access to the latest information.

T F 13. If investors form their forecasts using rational expectations, it is impossible to predict what the forecast error might be in the next period.

T F 14. If investors form their forecasts using rational expectations, it is impossible to predict anything about the next period.

T F 15. Under adaptive expectations, people learn from their past mistakes. However, under rational expectations, people learn from their future mistakes.

T F 16. If forecast errors under rational expectations have an average value of zero, then the best forecast for a security's future price is its current price.

T F 17. If markets are efficient and information set changes are random, then securities' prices will also change in accordance with these "random walks."

T F 18. If markets are efficient and market participants base their forecasts on rational expectations, then forecast errors will always be zero.

T F 19. If investors generally overreact and market prices consistently tend to swing too far up or too far down in the short-term, one could earn above average, risk-adjusted, excess returns by noting the overreaction and engaging in the opposite trade.

T F 20. Historically, under U.S. flow-of-funds analysis, the household sector has been a surplus spending unit (SSU).

T F 21. If the government sector of the economy moves from a deficit spending unit (DSU) to a surplus spending unit (SSU), then the business sector, household sector, non-U.S. sector, and financial sector must, in total, by definition, run net deficits.

T F 22. Under flow-of-funds analysis, borrowing must be equal to lending in each sector of the economy.

MULTIPLE CHOICE QUESTIONS

1. Expected short term interest rates are determined by all of the following except:
    a. expectations regarding long-term interest rates
    b. expectations regarding inflation
    c. expectations of changes in the money supply
    d. expectations regarding GDP

2. If market participants expect the money supply to increase in the future:
   a. present short-term rates are likely to fall
   b. long-term rates are likely to rise
   c. expected short-term rates are likely to fall
   d. expected short-term rates are likely to rise

3. If markets are efficient:
   a. returns on all securities are equivalent after adjusting for risk and liquidity
   b. one can earn above average returns only by accepting above average risk
   c. it is not possible to earn positive returns on investments
   d. all readily available information relevant to a security's return, risk, and liquidity is incorporated into that security's price
   e. a, b, and d

4. Which of the following statements is/are true?
   a. Adaptive expectations are, in part, forward looking.
   b. Rational expectations are, in part, forward looking.
   c. Rational expectations are never backward looking.
   d. All of the above statements are true.

5. Interest rates are based on expectations. Expectations, in turn, are based on:
   a. observations of past performance
   b. analysis of possible changes in the future
   c. random walks
   d. a and b

6. Assume that some part of the information set is too costly to include in the current assessment of securities prices. In such a case:
   a. markets can never be efficient
   b. markets must always be efficient
   c. markets are efficient if they incorporate the information that is available
   d. markets are only efficient if the prices determined in the marketplace do not differ from the prices that would be determined had the costly information been included

7. Suppose that long-term rates have risen, but short-term rates have not (i.e., the slope of the yield curve has grown more positive). Which of the following statements is most consistent with this observation?
   a. short-term rates are expected to fall
   b. corporate earnings are expected to fall
   c. corporate earnings are expected to increase
   d. inflation is expected to increase

8. If actual returns turn out, after the fact, to be different from expected returns:
   a. forecast errors are non-zero
   b. SSUs will be more satisfied with the results than will DSUs
   c. DSUs will be more satisfied with the results than will SSUs
   d. the household sector has most likely moved from being a surplus sector into being a deficit sector

9. If interest rates rise, but corporate earnings also rise:
   a. prices of stocks will fall
   b. the effect on stock prices is unclear
   c. prices of stocks will rise
   d. we are clearly just past the peak of the business cycle

10. Securities which have well developed secondary markets:
    a. have little liquidity risk
    b. will offer lower returns to investors, all else constant
    c. will be easier to issue in their primary markets
    d. all of the above

11. News comes out that makes the returns of virtually all financial assets more risky. Since this increased risk affects all the financial markets:
    a. the prices of virtually all securities will fall
    b. securities prices will remain stable as all assets have grown riskier by about the same degree
    c. the prices of virtually all securities will rise
    d. interest rates will remain stable

12. Assume that the household sector is net surplus. All remaining sectors are then, of course, in total, net deficit. If in the following period, the household sector moves to net deficit:
    a. interest rates are likely to rise to encourage the other sectors to increase their demand for loanable funds
    b. the entire economy will be net deficit
    c. interest rates are likely to rise to encourage the other sectors to increase their supply of loanable funds
    d. the government sector will certainly move to net surplus

13. All of the following unquestionably cast doubt on the rational expectations theory except:
    a. speculative bubbles
    b. overreactions
    c. the greater fool theory
    d. each of the above could be consistent with rational expectations

14. Assume that the average rate of return on a low-risk money market mutual fund is 4%. Further assume that the average rate of return on a fairly risky stock mutual fund is 20%. In such circumstances:
    a. the market is clearly not efficient
    b. the risk and liquidity adjusted returns of the two funds might still be equal
    c. an investor would clearly choose the 20% return stock fund
    d. the high returns of the stock mutual fund can not be sustained

15. If market participants expect an increase in the money supply and an increase in GDP growth:
    a. expected short-term rates are likely to rise
    b. long-term rates are likely to fall
    c. it is not clear if long-term rates are more likely to rise than to fall
    d. present short-term rates will likely rise

Chapter 7   Market Efficiency

16. If market participants expect a decrease in the money supply and a decrease in expected inflation:
    a. it is not clear if expected short-term rates are more likely to rise than to fall
    b. long-term rates can only remain stable
    c. it is not clear if long-term rates are more likely to rise than to fall
    d. present short-term rates can only remain stable
    e. a and c

17. All of the following statements correctly characterize efficient markets except:
    a. all financial instruments pay the same return
    b. prices of financial assets incorporate all publicly available information
    c. prices change quickly and accurately in response to information set changes
    d. prices reflect participants' expectations regarding future events

18. Which of the following is based both on past experience and analysis of possible future events?
    a. adaptive expectations
    b. unreasonable expectations
    c. unexciting expectations
    d. great expectations (my apologies to Charles Dickens)
    e. rational expectations

19. If households are in deficit and government is in deficit and non-financial businesses are in deficit and financial intermediaries are in balance then:
    a. interest rates must be at an all-time record high
    b. interest rates must be at all-time record low
    c. the non-U.S. sector must be in deficit
    d. the economy must be at a standstill
    e. the non-U.S. sector must be in surplus

20. If expected inflation is higher and expected GDP growth is higher:
    a. expected short-term rates are likely to rise
    b. long-term rates are likely to fall
    c. it is not clear if long-term rates are more likely to rise than to fall
    d. present short-term rates will likely fall

FILL IN QUESTIONS

1. _____ expectations are both forward looking and backward looking.

2. If interest rates are rising despite a slowing economy and an increasing money supply, then expected inflation must be _____.

3. In order for a market to be efficient, prices of financial assets must accurately reflect the _____ relevant to pricing the assets.

4. If people use adaptive expectations to form their opinions regarding future events, then those events that occurred _____ _____ will have the greatest impact on their forecasts.

5. In speculative bubbles, prices of financial assets disassociate from fundamental valuation concepts such as earnings and _____.

6. For each sector of the economy, _____ of funds and uses of funds must be equal.

7. For the economy as a whole, borrowing must be equal to _____.

8. In flow-of-funds analysis (ignoring the financial intermediaries sector), the economy is divided into four sectors: _____, _____, _____, and _____.

9. When prices are such that neither an excess supply of loanable funds is present nor is there excess demand for loanable funds, the financial markets are said to be _____.

10. If markets are efficient and expectations regarding relevant future events are rational, the _____ price of a security will be equal to the optimal _____ using all available information.

ESSAY QUESTIONS and INTERNET EXERCISES

1. Fischer Black once described Warren Buffett as a "five sigma event." What Dr. Black meant was that Mr. Buffett's investment savvy was, or, at least his investment results were, five standard deviations above that of the average investor. Now, if investment aptitude is roughly Normally distributed, then the chance of observing a outcome five standard deviations higher than the average is much, much less than one percent, less even than one-tenth of one percent. But, given that there are billions of people in the world, then, just by luck, every so often a Warren Buffett comes along. The market is still perfectly efficient (or, at least reasonably efficient). Mr. Buffett is just a very lucky guy. Examine Mr. Buffett's story at http://www.fool.com/specials/1999/sp990429Berkshire002.htm. Do you think Warren Buffett has earned long-term, above average, risk-adjusted, excess returns due to his savvy trades in an inefficient market? Or do you think that he is basically just a lucky guy?

2. Join the debate! Read over Dr. Robert Haugen's Web site - http://www.gsm.uci.edu/~haugen. Then read through the Investor Home Web site - http://www.investorhome.com/emh.htm. Okay, which is it? Are markets efficient? Or, are markets not efficient?

3. Go to the Federal Reserve's flow-of-funds Web site - http://www.federalreserve.gov/releases/Z1/Current. Select the "Summary statistics and table of contents" link. Read the summary and provide a short written interpretation of the major points.

8

How Exchange Rates Are Determined

SUMMARY

1. The exchange rate is the number of units of foreign money that can be acquired with one unit of domestic money. Students sometimes find the concept of pricing one currency in terms of another currency confusing. Perhaps we can bring clarity to the picture by first looking at price relationships with commodities that are familiar. For example, if one dollar buys twenty strawberries, the strawberry/dollar rate is 20 and the dollar/strawberry rate is 0.05. If steak costs eight dollars per pound, the steak/dollar rate is 0.125 and the dollar/steak rate is 8. We can carry the analogy further. The basic economic concepts – supply and demand – that determine the prices of strawberries and steak also determine the prices of yen and marks. We can perhaps pull one more insight from our strawberries and steak. Given the above prices, it must be true that one pound of steak is worth one hundred sixty strawberries (20 times 8). The steak/strawberry exchange rate must be 0.00625 and the strawberry/steak rate must be 160.

2. Continuing with the example from above, suppose the price of strawberries changes. One dollar now buys twenty-two strawberries. Are strawberries more expensive or less expensive? They are less expensive. We could just as well say that the dollar has appreciated against the strawberry. Why might this happen? Either the supply of strawberries has increased or the demand for strawberries has declined. Similarly, if one dollar buys one-half of a pound sterling (the U.K currency), so that the dollar/pound exchange rate is 2, but the next year one dollar buys two-thirds of a pound (the dollar/pound exchange rate is 1.5), has the dollar appreciated against the pound or depreciated against the pound? Are pounds cheaper or more expensive? Pounds are cheaper and the dollar has appreciated. (Concept check: suppose that bread went from $2.00 per loaf to $1.50 per loaf – has bread become cheaper or more expensive?)

3. What causes supply and demand for various currencies to change? The demand for dollars is a positive function of the demand by foreign consumers and investors for U.S. goods, services, and financial claims. If foreign consumers and investors demand more U.S. goods, then demand for dollars increases. The supply of dollars is a positive function of the demand by U.S. residents for foreign goods, services, and financial assets. If U.S. residents demand more foreign goods, the supply of dollars increases.

4. More precise statements of the demand for and supply of dollars can be gained from looking at the flow of dollars into or out of the currency exchange markets. In this context, demand for dollars per period is positively related to foreign income (a wealthier non-U.S. sector will have greater demand

for U.S. goods). Demand is also positively related to the foreign prices of foreign goods relative to the foreign prices of U.S. goods (if U.S. goods are cheaper, non-U.S. consumers will demand more of them). Demand is positively related to U.S. interest rates (if U.S. rates are high, foreigners will have a greater demand for U.S. financial assets). Demand for dollars is negatively related to the exchange rate itself (if the yen/dollar exchange rate rises from 100 to 150, the increased price of dollars in terms of yen will reduce Japanese consumer demand for U.S. goods).

5. Supply of dollars per period is positively related to U.S. income (as U.S. GDP rises, U.S. consumers will buy more of all goods and services, including foreign goods and services). Supply is positively related to the U.S. prices of U.S. goods relative to the U.S. prices of foreign goods (if U.S goods are relatively expensive, U.S. consumers will want more non-U.S. currency in order to purchase more non-U.S. goods). Supply is positively related to foreign interest rates (if non-U.S. rates are high, U.S. investors will want to purchase more foreign financial assets). Supply is positively related to the exchange rate itself (if the yen/dollar rate rises from 100 to 150, the reduced price of yen in terms of dollars will increase U.S. consumer demand for Japanese goods).

6. The dollar will depreciate when (examining each in turn while holding all other factors constant): U.S. interest rates fall relative to non-U.S. interest rates, U.S income rises, non-U.S. income falls, and U.S inflation is above non-U.S inflation. The dollar appreciates when (again imposing the ceteris paribus conditions): U.S interest rates rise relative to non-U.S. rates, U.S. income falls, non-U.S. income rises, and U.S. inflation is less than non-U.S. inflation.

7. Currency flows between nations are recorded, in effect, in the balance of payments accounts. The balance of payments record has two main accounts – the current account and the capital account. By definition, any surplus or deficit in the current account will be "balanced" by a deficit or surplus in the capital account. Changes in the current and capital accounts can reveal probable changes in currency exchange rates. For example, if U.S. interest rates rise relative to non-U.S. rates, capital will flow into the U.S. and the U.S. will show a capital surplus and, by necessity in order to make the balance of payments balance, a current account deficit. The dollar will appreciate and U.S goods will become more expensive to non-U.S. consumers, accentuating the current account deficit as fewer U.S. goods are shipped overseas. Eventually, as demand for U.S. goods softens, the U.S. economy will slow, U.S. interest rates will fall, and the capital surplus will become smaller. This is to say that exchange rate adjustments are an important part of bringing current and capital flows into equilibrium. Countries with current account deficits are said to have a trade deficit. But it should be kept in mind that any country with a trade deficit has, by definition, an offsetting capital surplus.

8. Purchasing power parity holds when, in equilibrium (i.e., when exchange rates adjust such that the supply of dollars and the demand for dollars are equal), the relative purchasing power of currencies is equal. Thus, ignoring taxes, tariffs, and other restrictions on trade, and assuming that all goods are viewed as equally attractive (or unattractive) by all consumers worldwide, a cheeseburger in the U.S. will sell for the same price as does a cheeseburger in Japan, once we've adjusted for the exchange rate. If the yen/dollar rate is 100, and a cheeseburger in the U.S. costs $2.00, that same quality cheeseburger will sell for 200 yen in Japan. And if we could establish the currency exchange rate between the U.S. and paradise, purchasing power parity would allow us to find the price of that lyrical "cheeseburger in paradise."

TRUE/FALSE QUESTIONS

T F 1. Holding all other factors constant, if U.S. interest rates rise, the U.S. trade deficit will grow larger.

T F 2. If purchasing power parity holds, all currencies are equal in value. Thus, a video game that sells for $10 in the U.S. will sell for 10 yen in Japan.

T F 3. As the U.S. economy grows, holding all other factors constant, the dollar is likely to appreciate against non-U.S. currencies.

T F 4. If the yen/dollar exchange rate is 128, the dollar/yen rate must be 0.128.

T F 5. The economies of nations with trade deficits (i.e., deficits in their current accounts) can never be expanding.

T F 6. With regard to the balance of payments, most nations design monetary and fiscal policies that attempt to allow them to obtain simultaneous surpluses in both their current account and their capital account.

T F 7. If the dollar/yen exchange rate moves from 128 to 123, holding all other factors constant, the demand for dollars to flow into the dollar–yen exchange market will fall.

T F 8. If the Federal Reserve takes actions to increase the money supply, and assuming that expected inflation in the U.S. nonetheless remains stable, the dollar is likely to rise in value relative to non-U.S. currencies.

T F 9. If the peso/dollar exchange rate is 9.25 and the Swiss Franc/dollar rate is 1.65, one Swiss Franc costs less than 5.5 pesos.

T F 10. If the peso/dollar exchange rate moves from 9.5 to 9.25, the supply of dollars into the peso – dollar currency exchange market will increase.

T F 11. When the prices of U.S. goods rise relative to the dollar price of non-U.S. goods, the supply of dollars in the currency exchange markets will increase.

T F 12. If the Japanese economy slows, holding all other factors constant, the yen is likely to appreciate against the dollar.

T F 13. If the U.S. becomes a less-attractive place for non-U.S. investors to invest, the U.S. trade deficit will narrow and, potentially, even go into surplus.

T F 14. High inflation in the United States will cause the dollar to appreciate against most world currencies.

T F 15. If the dollar/yen exchange rate moves from 0.008197 to 0.007936, the dollar has appreciated against the yen.

T F   16.   In general, financial assets of nations that are running trade deficits are viewed as unattractive investments by investors outside that nation.

T F   17.   If U.S. consumer demand for Canadian goods and services rises, the value of the Canadian dollar will fall relative to the U.S. dollar.

T F   18.   If non-U.S. investors begin to sell off a substantial portion of their U.S. financial assets, the U.S. capital account is likely to move from a surplus to a deficit (holding all other factors constant).

T F   19.   If non-U.S. investors begin to sell off a substantial portion of their U.S. financial assets, the U.S. dollar will likely appreciate relative to world currencies (holding all other factors constant).

T F   20.   Suppose that a U.S. consumer expects the yen/dollar exchange rate to go from 125 to 122 in the near future. Holding all else constant, the U.S. consumer would be more likely to wait a bit before buying that new Japanese-manufactured Toyota.

T F   21.   I wish I was still pricing strawberries and steak (see Summary above) rather than these %$#^7**&& currencies.

MULTIPLE CHOICE QUESTIONS

1. Suppose that the typical basket of goods and services purchased during a typical month in Tokyo costs 384,000 yen. If purchasing power parity holds and the dollar/yen exchange rate is 128, in the U.S. this basket of goods and services will cost:
   a. $49,152,000
   b. $ 128,000
   c. $ 3,000
   d. $ 2,125

2. If the Swedish krona/ U.S. dollar exchange rate is 10.5 and a U.S. based company needs 3,250,00 krona to purchase a Swedish telephone switch center, how many dollars will the U.S. firm spend on the center?
   a. $34,125,000
   b. $ 309,524
   c. $ 256,694
   d. $ 44,800

3. If the yen/dollar exchange rate moves form 128 to 133, the dollar is said to have:
   a. appreciated relative to the yen
   b. depreciated relative to the yen
   c. reached parity with the yen
   d. eliminated the trade deficit with the Japan

4. Assume purchasing power parity holds. Further assume that the yen/dollar exchange rate is 125. If a Nissan sedan costs 3,875,000 yen in Tokyo, that same car will sell for what price in Los Angeles?
   a. $22,500
   b. $25,500
   c. $27,850
   d. $31,000

5. Assume purchasing power parity holds. Further assume that the yen/dollar exchange rate is 125. Also assume that the Euro/dollar exchange rate is 1.10. If a Nissan sedan costs 3,875,000 yen in Tokyo, that same car will sell for what price in Frankfurt?
   a. €4,262,500
   b. €   440,341
   c. €   34,100
   d. €   28,182

6. Which of the following is likely to increase the demand for dollars in the currency exchange market?
   a. a fall in non-U.S. incomes
   b. falling U.S. interest rates
   c. U.S. goods selling for lower prices in foreign markets
   d. none of the above

7. If the United States takes actions to reduce its trade deficit:
   a. the dollar might nevertheless appreciate
   b. the capital account surplus will fall
   c. U.S. interest rates might nevertheless rise
   d. none of the above

8. Which of the following is likely to increase the supply of dollars in the currency exchange market?
   a. a fall in U.S. incomes
   b. increasing non-U.S. interest rates
   c. foreign goods selling for higher prices in U.S. markets
   d. none of the above

9. If the U.S. current account is in deficit against the rest of the world, while the Japanese capital account is in deficit with the rest of the world:
   a. Japan must be running a trade deficit
   b. the U.S. must be running a trade deficit
   c. the world's aggregate balance of payments must not be in balance
   d. none of the above

10. If the U.S. current account is in deficit against the rest of the world, while the Japanese capital account is in deficit with the rest of the world:
    a. Japan is effectively supplying the U.S. with investment capital

b. U.S. ownership of non-U.S. financial assets must be increasing, in net
c. the balance of payments solely between the U.S. and Japan must be in balance
d. all of the above

11. In early 2001, the U.S. economy appeared to have weakened. Holding other factors constant, this suggests:
    a. the value of the U.S. dollar will stabilize
    b. the value of the U.S. dollar will rise
    c. the value of the U.S. dollar will fall
    d. none of the above

12. If the interest rates of financial assets denominated in Euros increase relative to U.S. interest rates:
    a. the Euro is likely to appreciate versus the dollar
    b. the dollar is likely to appreciate versus the Euro
    c. U.S. interest rates will likely fall in response to such an increase in Euro rates
    d. purchasing power parity between the dollar and the Euro will be less likely to hold

13. Suppose you are an American investor and you've recently purchased a bond denominated in Korean won.
    a. You are afraid of the won appreciating against the dollar.
    b. You are afraid of the won remaining stable against the dollar.
    c. You are afraid of the won depreciating against the dollar.
    d. You aren't afraid of anything.

14. If Japanese interest rates rise relative to U.S interest rates, but Japanese interest rates fall relative to Korean interest rates:
    a. the Korean won is likely to strengthen against the Japanese yen
    b. the Korean won is likely to strengthen against the U.S. dollar
    c. the Korean capital account is likely to show either a reduced deficit or an increased surplus, ceteris paribus
    d. all of the above
    e. none of the above

15. If U.S. consumers increase their demand for non-U.S. goods and services:
    a. the dollar is likely to appreciate
    b. the value of the dollar will be unaffected so long as the non-U.S. goods and services are priced in currencies other than the dollar
    c. the dollar is likely to depreciate
    d. non-U.S. consumers will, in turn, immediately increase their demand for U.S. goods and services

Chapter 8 — How Exchange Rates Are Determined

FILL IN QUESTIONS

1. In the early 1990s, the Federal Reserve pursued a relatively easy monetary policy and U.S. interest rates fell. This explains, at least in part, why the dollar _____ during this period.

2. Holding all else constant, investors are more likely to invest in financial assets denominated in U.S. dollars if U.S. interest rates are relatively _____.

3. If expected inflation in the United States is greater, the U.S. dollar is more likely to _____ relative to non-U.S. currencies.

4. If the U.S. current account is in deficit against the rest of the world, the U.S. capital account must be in _____.

5. As foreign interest rates rise relative to U.S. interest rates, the _____ dollars will increase.

6. Suppose that the yen/dollar exchange rate is expected to go from 125 to 122 in the near future. Holding all else constant, this would make a Japanese investor _____ likely to purchase a U.S Treasury bond.

7. The theory that holds that in the long run all goods and services are equally priced after the proper currency exchange rate adjustments are made is the _____ theory.

8. As foreign real incomes rise, demand for dollars in the currency exchange market will _____, holding all other factors constant.

9. As the dollar prices of U.S. goods _____ relative to the dollar prices of non-U.S. goods, the supply of dollars into the currency exchange market will decline.

10. The quantity demanded of dollars is _____ related to the exchange rate.

ESSAY QUESTIONS

1. Although in the real world it is almost never possible to hold all other things constant, (the famous "ceteris paribus" conditions), economists are constantly imposing such conditions on their analyses. Why? Why not study how all things respond to all things simultaneously?

2. Over the recent past, much has been made of the trade deficits that the U.S runs against the rest of the world. Has your study of currency exchange rates influenced the importance you attach to these trade deficits?

3. This chapter abstracts somewhat from reality by ignoring transactions costs of trading in the currency exchange markets. When we factor in the bid-ask spread of currency dealers, we find, for example, that we have "bands" of exchange rates (bounded by the bid prices and the ask prices) rather than precise exchange rates. Holding all else constant (here we go again!), would the size of these bid-ask spreads affect the supply/demand functions driving exchange rates towards equilibrium?

INTERNET EXERCISES

1. Bloomberg provides currency quotes and an exchange rate calculator at http://www.bloomberg.com/markets/currency.html. Click on the "Cross Currency" link and you'll see a matrix of exchange rates for major world currencies. Read down the "USD" column to the "GBP" row. That's the British pound/U.S. dollar exchange rate. Then read across the "USD" row until you are under the "GBP" column. That's the dollar/pound rate. Are the two rates related? Take the inverse of one of the rates. What do you get? Use your "Back" button to return to the previous screen. Can you find the exchange rate between dollars and the Peruvian new sol by clicking on the appropriate link? How about the rate between dollars and the Estonian kroon?

2. A Canadian currency-trading firm (Customhouse Currency Exchange) will try to entice you into trading through them if you go to their Web site - http://www.customhouse.com. I thought their "Trading Demo" program was well worth a look. After getting into the demo program, click on "Basic Trade." Try to **sell** $100,000 U.S. for yen. Proceed through the demo until you get to "Your Rate." Write this number down. Then "Cancel" the trade, which will take you back to the earlier screen. Now enter an order to **buy** $100,000 by selling yen. Work your way through to the "Your Rate" screen. Compare this number to the previous number. Why are the numbers different? Who could have imagined twenty years ago that losing money in currency transactions could be so easy and convenient? Right from the comfort of your own den or living room! Of course, I suppose it is possible to make money. But watch out for that bid-ask spread!

9

The Money Market

SUMMARY

1. The term 'money market' refers to financial markets where short-term, large denomination financial assets are traded. Money markets are highly liquid and money market instruments have little default risk. Major issuers of money market instruments include: the U.S. Treasury, U.S. federal government sponsored enterprises (GSEs), state and local governments, non-financial businesses, and financial businesses (did I leave anybody out?). Purchasers of money market instruments include banks and savings associations, GSEs, the Federal Reserve (buying and selling T-bills to put into effect monetary policy), non-financial businesses, pension funds, insurance companies, brokerage houses, money market mutual funds (MMMFs), and individuals. Purchases of money market instruments are motivated, often enough, because of a temporary mismatch of funds flowing into an entity versus funds flowing out, rather than being motivated by the potential return, per se, of the money market instrument. Purchasers buy money market instruments to earn a (slightly) higher return than can be realized by holding actual cash, but want the money market instruments to be almost as liquid as cash (nearly as liquid as money itself, hence the name). Liquidity and low risk are the primary motivations for purchasing money market instruments; rate of return is secondary.

2. Money market instruments include: commercial paper, Federal funds, repurchase agreements, negotiable certificates of deposit (CDs), Treasury bills, Eurodollar instruments, and bankers' acceptances. Treasury bills are pure discount, short-term instruments issued by the U.S. Treasury. Typical maturities are 3 months and 6 months. They pay no coupons, paying only their face value at maturity. Thus, they always sell at a discount to their maturity value, with this discount representing the interest earned on the bill. T-bills are free of default risk and highly liquid. Commercial paper is issued by creditworthy corporations. Typical maturities are less then 9 months. Commercial paper does not pay coupons and, therefore, is always sold at a discount to its maturity value. Fed funds are bank reserves on deposit with the Federal Reserve system that may be lent overnight from banks with too many reserves to banks with too few. To sell a security (usually a T-bill) and agree to repurchase it tomorrow at a slightly higher price is to enter into a repurchase agreement (repo). A repo is a means for the seller (who is also the repurchaser) of the security to borrow money short term. The slightly higher price represents interest paid on the loan. The party opposite the seller/repurchaser is said to have entered into a reverse repo. Negotiable CDs are short-term CDs issued by banks and are distinguished from other CDs in that negotiable CDs have a secondary market (i.e., they can be sold prior to their maturity). Eurodollar CDs are dollar-denominated negotiable CDs issued by banks outside of the U.S. Nobody knows what bankers' acceptances are (just kidding, just kidding). BAs are used to facilitate international trade. A bank that "accepts" the BA is guaranteeing timely payment on the note, which is generally the obligation of an importer to pay for goods shipped from abroad. BAs have declined in importance with the increased globalization of international banks, as

more businesses are now willing to accept credit card payments and even checks from foreign customers or suppliers.

3. Money market mutual funds are open-ended investment companies (mutual funds) that invest solely in money market instruments. Mutual funds pool the investments of thousand of relatively small investors. MMMFs provide small investors the opportunity to participate in the money market. MMMFs can be viewed as checking accounts that pay interest, except that the number of checks one can write per month on a MMMF is limited to three.

4. The interest rate earned (or paid) on a money market instrument can be calculated as:

Interest rate = [(ending value – beginning value) / beginning value] * (360 / Δ days)

where Δ days stands for the number of days the instrument is held (often the number of days to maturity). For T-bills substitute 365 for 360 in the above and use the par value of the bill as the ending value in order to calculate the bill's "bond equivalent yield."

5. Treasury bills are quoted using discount yields. The formula relating these discount yields to the price of the bill is:

T-bill discount = [(Par – Purchase price) / Par] * (360 / n)

where n stands for the number of days until maturity.

TRUE/FALSE QUESTIONS

T F 1. Commercial paper represents short-term debt obligations of, for the most part, businesses with substantial credit risk.

T F 2. Treasury bills always sell at a discount from their maturity value.

T F 3. A commercial bank short of reserves might often borrow additional reserves through the fed funds market or enter into repurchase agreements to obtain short-term loans, with the proceeds of the loan deposited as reserves with the Federal Reserve.

T F 4. By entering into a reverse repo, one is, in effect, lending money.

T F 5. Negotiable CDs are low risk instruments because the entire face value of the CD is guaranteed by the Federal Deposit Insurance Corporation (FDIC).

T F 6. Money market instruments are almost as liquid as money itself.

T F 7. The minimum maturity value for Treasury bills is $10,000.

T F 8. MMMFs are negotiable CDs issued by large money-center commercial banks.

T F 9. MMMF growth in the late 1970s was fueled by the inability of banks to raise interest rates to competitive levels due to the interest rate ceilings imposed on banks by the Federal Reserve Board's "Regulation Q."

T F 10. Disintermediation occurs when investors remove funds from financial intermediaries such as commercial banks and invest those funds directly with issuers of securities.

T F 11. In the early 1980s, Congress deregulated interest rate ceilings that had been imposed on banks and the money market mutual fund business soon thereafter shrank to a fraction of its former size.

T F 12. The fed funds rate is the rate paid by the U.S. federal government on the Treasury obligations that it issues.

T F 13. One attractive feature of the repurchase agreement market is that, to date, there has never been a major default by any participant in the market.

T F 14. While no money market instruments are included in M1, some are included in M2, M3, and DNFD.

T F 15. Finance companies such as GMAC issue large amounts of commercial paper and use the proceeds primarily to make consumer loans.

T F 16. In auctioning Treasury bills, the Treasury separates bids into competitive bids and noncompetitive bids.

T F 17. When the Treasury receives a "noncompetitive" bid during the T-bill auction process, it notifies the bidder that the bid is too low (i.e., it is noncompetitive with other bids).

T F 18. Eurodollar instruments are denominated in Euros.

T F 19. Many money market instruments (and those of other markets as well), reference LIBOR, even though the instruments trade outside of London, England.

T F 20. Money market instruments are only denominated in U.S. dollars.

T F 21. Although MMMFs have allowed individual investors to participate in the money market, the high initial minimum investments, typically in excess of $100,000, keep most Americans from being able to purchase MMMFs.

T F 22. MMMFs are fully insured by the FDIC.

T F 23. A large proportion of U.S. federal debt is actually held by the U.S. government itself, primarily through the Social Security Trust Funds.

T F 24. Eurodollar instruments are dollar denominated financial assets issued solely by banks in London, England.

MULTIPLE CHOICE QUESTIONS

1. All of the following are money market instruments except:
   a. Treasury bonds
   b. Treasury bills
   c. Eurodollar CDs
   d. federal funds

2. Money market instruments share all of the following qualities except:
   a. high liquidity
   b. large denominations
   c. high returns
   d. low risk

3. A money market mutual fund would be unlikely to purchase:
   a. commercial paper
   b. Treasury bills
   c. reverse repo
   d. federal funds

4. Calculate the purchase price of a $1,000,000 par value Treasury bill given that the bill has 84 days to maturity and a quoted discount yield of 4%.
   a. $1,166,617
   b. $1,000,000
   c. $ 999,975
   d. $ 990,667

5. Find the bond equivalent yield of a $10,000 par value Treasury bill that is currently selling for $9,889, given that the bill has 127 days to maturity.
   a. 4.56%
   b. 3.23%
   c. 2.11%
   d. 0.99%

6. If commercial paper with 181 days to maturity is selling for 97.75% of its par value, the implied repo rate on the paper is (hint: use equation 9-2 from the text, using 100 as the selling price):
   a. 4.58%
   b. 3.23%
   c. 2.11%
   d. 1.09%

7. A 91-day Treasury bill is selling for 96.5% of par value. What is the quoted discount yield on the bill?
   a. 14.35%
   b. 14.00%
   c. 13.85%
   d. 3.5%

Chapter 9 The Money Market

8. Which of the following money market instruments has the most active secondary market?
   a. bankers' acceptances
   b. negotiable CDs
   c. commercial paper
   d. U.S. Treasury bills

9. Which of the following is correct?
   a. banks and saving associations are the largest issuers of Treasury bills
   b. casualty and property insurers are more likely to use money market instruments as part of their investment strategy than are life insurers
   c. the Federal open market committee (FOMC) primarily executes monetary policy by buying or selling federal funds
   d. none of the above

10. Which of the following is correct?
    a. the auction process used by the Treasury to sell T-bills ensures that competitive bids will receive the number of T-bills they request
    b. individual investors cannot purchase T-bills directly from the government; rather, they must use one of the thirty or so approved government T-bill dealers to process their orders
    c. the auction process used by the Treasury to sell T-bills ensures that noncompetitive bids will receive the number of T-bills they request
    d. all of the above

11. Calculate the bond equivalent yield of the following T-bill. The T-bill has 12 days to maturity and is selling for 99.8975% of par.
    a. 27.34%
    b. 10.00%
    c. 3.12%
    d. 1.14%

12. All of the following would constitute money market transactions except:
    a. commercial banks borrowing in the federal funds market
    b. commercial banks lending in the federal funds market
    c. insurance companies entering into a reverse repo with a stockbrokerage house
    d. all of the above are money market transactions

13. All of the following are government sponsored entities except:
    a. Fannie Mae
    b. Sallie Mae
    c. Freddie Mac
    d. Rural Pa

14. Which of the following is correct?
    a. T-bills have slightly more default risk then do financial assets issued by GSEs
    b. Ginnie Mae bonds have less default risk than corporate commercial paper
    c. bankers' acceptances are slightly more liquid than are T-bills
    d. all of the above
    e. none of the above

15. You would be very surprised to see which of the following entities attempting to borrow in the Federal funds market.
    a. the Federal Reserve Bank of New York
    b. Bank of America
    c. J.P Morgan Chase & Co.
    d. Citibank

FILL IN QUESTIONS

1. The interest rate charged on overnight loans between member banks of the British Bankers' Association is called _____.

2. Individual investors are able to participate in money market investments by buying and selling _____.

3. When individuals withdraw funds from financial intermediaries such as commercial banks and place those funds directly with issuers such as the U.S. Treasury, the process is known as _____.

4. The Federal Reserve's open market committee puts into effect monetary policy primarily by buying or selling _____.

5. If investor X agrees to purchase securities today and sell them back to a the other party tomorrow for a slightly higher price, investor X has entered into a _____.

6. The money market instrument with the most active, most liquid secondary market is _____.

7. Instruments that pay no coupon always sell _____ maturity value and are often referred to as pure _____ instruments.

8. _____ are large denomination money market instruments issued by banks (note: this question does not refer to commercial paper issued by bank holding corporations).

9. Foreign CDs issued in the U.S. are known as _____ CDs.

10. If the Federal government continues to run unified budget surpluses, the amount of Treasury bills held by the public is likely to _____.

ESSAY QUESTIONS and INTERNET EXERCISES

1. Check the latest Treasury bill auction results at - http://www.treasurydirect.gov. Look in the column on the left side of the site and click on "Auction Information" under "T-Bills, Notes and Bonds." Then click on "Recent Treasury Bill Auction Results Table." Open a new window in your browser and go to - http://www.federalreserve.gov/releases/cp - which is the Federal Reserve Web site that reports commercial paper rates. Which rates are higher? Make certain you compare discount rates to discount rates for instruments of approximately the same maturity. Also, remember that the greater the discount, the lower the price. Use the formula in summary point 5 above to calculate the price of one of the T-bills and one of the commercial paper issues. Use a par value of 100. Then convert the discount quotes to bond equivalent yields using the formula in summary point 4. Remember to substitute 365 for 360. Which instrument has the higher bond equivalent yield?

2. Take a trip to Jamaica (well, a virtual trip). Go to - http://www.jmmb.com - a Jamaican money market dealer. Click on "Market Information." Then click on "Money Market Bulletin." Are Jamaican money market rates higher than those in the U.S.? Why? And if you like those high rates, before you rush off to buy Government of Jamaica Treasury bills, re-read Chapter 8. (Hint: what must be the relationship between expected inflation in Jamaica and expected inflation in the U.S.?)

10

The Corporate and Government Bond Markets

SUMMARY

1. Bonds are debt obligations issued by domestic and foreign corporations, the federal government, government sponsored enterprises, foreign governments, and state and local governments. Bonds repay investors through periodic payments called coupons and a terminating payment at maturity. The maturity payment is also known as par value, face value, nominal value, stated value, contract value, and has several more synonyms as well. The annual coupon payments can be found by multiplying the par value of the bond by the coupon rate stated on the instrument. If coupons are paid semi-annually, as is often the case with bonds issued in the U.S., one-half of the annual coupon is paid every six months. Zero coupon bonds pay a maturity payment only.

2. Most bonds issued in the U.S. are registered bonds; the coupon check will be mailed to the registered owner. Bearer bonds have paper coupons attached to the bond; the coupons are clipped off and presented for payment in a fashion similar to the check clearing process. The holder of a bearer bond is presumed to be the owner of the bond. Bonds are rated by Moody's and Standard & Poor's as to default risk. The obligations the bond issuer has to the bond purchasers are spelled out in the bond indenture. Bond trustees, mostly commercial banks, ensure that the provisions of the indenture are followed. Mortgage bonds are backed by real estate property. Debenture bonds are not backed by specific collateral. In the event of default, subordinated debentures are only paid after more senior debentures have been paid.

3. Treasury bonds are issued by the U.S. Treasury. They can be purchased from a securities dealer, bank, or directly from the Federal Reserve. The secondary market for Treasury bonds is the most active in the world. The coupons and the maturity payment on Treasury bonds can be "stripped" from the bond and sold as separate instruments. These STRIPS are then separate zero coupon bonds. STRIPS trade actively. Inflation-protected bonds have been less successful. Inflation protected bonds have their coupon and maturity payments indexed for inflation.

4. Municipal bonds are issued by state and local governments. Interest income on municipals is exempt from federal taxes, making them attractive investments for high tax-bracket investors. Municipal general obligation bonds are repaid from any revenue (tax) source available to the issuer. Revenue bonds, on the other hand, are repaid solely from the revenues generated by the project built with the proceeds of the bond. For example, a sewer district revenue bond would rely on the revenues generated by homes tapping into the sewer and monthly sewerage fees to repay bonds issued to build the sewer.

5. The value of a bond is the present value of the coupons and maturity payments discounted at the appropriate interest rate for the bond's risk and maturity. When interest rates rise, the price of the bond declines, and vice-versa. The discount rate applied to the bond's cash flows is called the bond's yield to maturity (YTM). The YTM of the bond depends on the shape of the yield curve and the risk premium appropriate to the bond. The risk premium depends on economy wide factors such as expected inflation, monetary policy, and economic growth. Company specific factors such as the capital structure of the firm and the firm's credit rating also impact the risk premium.

6. When using a financial calculator to value (price) bonds, enter the bond's coupon rate into the "PMT" key (use one-half the coupon rate for semi-annual bonds), enter the number of years into "N" (use twice the number of years for semi-annual bonds), enter the YTM into the "I/YR" (use one-half the YTM for semi-annual bonds), and put 100 into "FV." Calculate "PV" – that's the price of the bond expressed in percent of par. It's negative as it represents the outflow of funds to buy the bond, with the coupons and maturity value being positive cash flows.

7. Callable bonds can be paid early by the issuer. If interest rates decline, issuers will issue new low coupon bonds and use the proceeds to retire (call) existing high coupon debt. Investors don't like calls, as they must give up their high coupon bonds and can reinvest the proceeds only into low coupon issues. Sinking funds allow the issuer to partially redeem the bonds each year. Thus reduces the "crisis at maturity," which occurs when issuers are unable to pay the maturity value of the bond. A convertible bond can be converted into a set number of shares of stock.

TRUE/FALSE QUESTIONS

T F 1. Callable bonds are more likely to be called if prevailing interest rates are now higher than were the rates at the time the bond was issued.

T F 2. As interest rates increase, the prices of existing bonds fall.

T F 3. As interest rates change, the present values of cash flows further into the future change more than the present values of nearby cash flows. Thus, the greater the maturity of a bond, holding all other factors constant, the greater the price changes of the bond in response to interest rate changes.

T F 4. One risk faced by bondholders is the risk that they will be unable to reinvest the coupons paid on a bond into financial assets that pay attractive interest rates. Such reinvestment is a necessary part of the compound interest assumption. However, zero coupon bonds, having no coupons to reinvest, have no reinvestment risk.

T F 5. If interest rates increase, the coupons paid by a bond could be reinvested at the higher rates increasing one's return. However, zero coupon bonds have no coupons that could be reinvested. Thus, zero coupon bonds are more exposed to loss of value should rates increase than are coupon bonds.

T F 6. A taxpayer in the 27% tax bracket would prefer a tax-exempt municipal paying 5% interest to a corporate bond paying 7.5% interest, all else held constant.

T F   7. U.S. Treasury bonds pay coupons semi-annually.

T F   8. Treasury STRIPS are default free, zero coupon bonds.

T F   9. The most liquid bond market in the world is the market for U.S. Treasury bonds.

T F   10. A bond with more default risk would pay a higher risk premium.

T F   11. Generally speaking, the higher a firm's leverage ratio, the greater the risk of default faced by the firm's bondholders.

T F   12. Convertible bonds allow bondholders to defer receipt of coupons, thus converting the coupons into capital gains that are taxed at a lower rate than the tax rate applied to coupons.

T F   13. Sinking fund provisions require bond issuers to pay off (retire) a portion of the outstanding bonds each year.

T F   14. Treasury STRIPS always sell at discounts to their maturity values.

T F   15. Assume that a bond issued four years ago has a coupon rate of 5.5%. If the appropriate discount rate to apply to the bond's cash flows is now 6.25%, the bond will sell for a price below its par value.

T F   16. In general, one would expect bonds issued by Fannie Mae to carry higher risk premiums than bonds with similar coupons and maturities issued by a U.S. corporation, say IBM.

T F   17. Holding all other factors constant, a bond with a higher coupon rate will sell for a lower price.

T F   18. Eurobonds are dollar denominated bonds issued outside the United States.

T F   19. Compared to the historical record, the debt of U.S. nonfinancial firms is now a relatively high proportion of U.S. GDP.

T F   20. The debt of U.S. nonfinancial firms relative to the market values of those firms is currently low in comparison to the historical level of this leverage ratio.

T F   21. Treasury bonds are without risk.

T F   22. You would be astounded if a government sponsored enterprise, such as Fannie Mae, issued junk bonds.

T F   23. Debenture bonds are backed by specific collateral such as plant and equipment or inventory.

T F   24. Indentures are placed into one's mouth by an indentist.

MULTIPLE CHOICE QUESTIONS

1. Which of the following bonds would have the least reinvestment rate risk:
   a. an 8% coupon, twenty year Fannie Mae bond
   b. a July 2009 Treasury STRIP
   c. a 4% coupon, thirty year GM subordinated debenture
   d. a 16% coupon, ten year bond issued by We-Sell-Junk Financial

2. A bond with a par value of $1,000 and a coupon rate of 6%, coupons paid semi-annually, would pay a coupon of:
   a. $30 once per year
   b. $ 6 once per year
   c. $30 twice per year
   d. $60 once per year

3. A bond with ten years to maturity has a coupon rate of 5%, coupons paid semi-annually, and a par value of $1,000. If the YTM on the bond is 6%, the price of the bond is:
   a. $1,004.56
   b. $1,000.00
   c. $ 925.61
   d. $ 687.75

4. A bond has a coupon rate of 5% and a par value of $1,000. The bond's YTM is also 5%. The price of the bond is:
   a. $1,166
   b. $1,000
   c. $ 975
   d. more information is needed to answer this question

5. Holding all other factors constant, which of the following presents in correct order, from highest return to lowest return, the expected returns on these classes of bonds:
   a. mortgage bonds, debenture bonds, subordinated debenture bonds
   b. debenture bonds, mortgage bonds, Treasury bonds
   c. debenture bonds, subordinated debenture bonds, Treasury bonds
   d. Treasury bonds, subordinated debenture bonds, mortgage bonds

6. Calculate the YTM of the following bond. The bond has two years left to maturity, a par value of $1,000, a coupon rate of 5%, and it pays its coupons semi-annually. The bond currently sells for $981.41. (Hint: find the present value of the bond's cash flows using each of the rates given below until you find the rate that makes the present value of the bond equal to $981.41. The bond has semi-annual coupons, so remember to double the number of years, use one-half the stated YTM, and use one-half the annual coupon.)
   a. 6%
   b. 5%
   c. 4%
   d. 3%

Chapter 10 The Corporate and Government Bond Markets

7. What is the value of a Treasury STRIP that promises to pay $100,000 in exactly five years, if the appropriate rate of interest to use in discounting the STRIP's cash flow is 6%, compounded semi-annually?
   a. $134,392
   b. $100,000
   c. $ 74,409
   d. $ 6,000

8. All of the following are government sponsored enterprises except:
   a. the Ohio Lottery
   b. the TVA
   c. Ginnie Mae
   d. the Farm Credit System

9. The U.S. Treasury recently suspended issuance of new thirty-year Treasury bonds. This is most likely due to:
   a. the continuing budget deficits of the federal government
   b. the high coupon rates required of such bonds in order to make them competitive with U.S. corporate issues
   c. the reluctance of Republican administrations to reduce federal spending
   d. the consolidated budget surpluses the federal government has had over the recent few years

10. If the slope of the yield curve steepens, so that long term rates are now much higher than short term rates, and assuming that short-term rates hardly changed at all, which of the following bonds would change the most in price?
    a. a two year, 16% coupon junk bond
    b. a thirty-year, zero coupon AA rated corporate bond
    c. a one-year Treasury STRIP
    d. none of the above would change in price by a significant amount

11. Which of the following is likely to result in bond ratings of Baa (Moody's) or BBB (Standard & Poor's) or lower:
    a. the issuing firm has experienced net losses
    b. the issuing firm has increased its leverage
    c. the issuing firm has missed some loan payments
    d. all of the above
    e. none of the above

12. Using the Standard and Poor's rating system, the highest rated bonds have ratings of:
    a. AAAA
    b. AAA
    c. AA
    d. A

13. All of the following are terms that relate to a discussion of corporate bonds except:
    a. indenture
    b. restrictive covenant
    c. debenture
    d. insubordination
    e. all of the above terms relate to corporate bonds

14. Which of the following bonds will sell below par value?
    a. an 8% coupon bond with six years to maturity that has a YTM of 7%
    b. a thirty-year corporate bond with a YTM of 5% and a coupon of 6.25%
    c. a Treasury bond with five years to maturity, a coupon of 6%, and a YTM of 6%
    d. all of the above
    e. none of the above

15. If economic conditions increase the potential for default, which of the following is most likely to *increase* in price?
    a. a 6% U.S. Treasury bond with 12 years to maturity
    b. a BBB rated corporate bond with 10 years to maturity and a coupon of 14%
    c. a Ba rated corporate bond with 14 years to maturity and a 5% coupon, which is currently callable at a call price of 103 percent of par
    d. an AAA rated zero coupon corporate bond with forty years to maturity

16. Which of the following factors affect the risk-free rate?
    a. changes in capital inflows
    b. changes in inflationary expectations
    c. changes in government borrowing
    d. all of the above
    e. none of the above

17. Which of the following factors affect the risk premium?
    a. the economic outlook
    b. the credit rating of the bond
    c. the capital structure of the firm
    d. all of the above
    e. none of the above

FILL IN QUESTIONS

1. If interest rates increase, the prices of most bonds will _____.

2. Although some older bearer bonds still exist, essentially all bonds now issued in the U.S. are issued as _____ bonds.

3. Bonds rated Ba or lower by Moody's or BB or lower by Standard & Poor's are called _____ bonds.

4. The separate trading of registered interest and principal allows investors purchasing _____ to invest in zero coupon, default free, Treasury debt.

5. A bond that has its coupons and principal adjusted for inflation is known as an _____ _____ bond.

6. If the general taxing authority of a municipal issuer is available to pay the coupons and maturity of a bond, the bond is said to be a _____ bond.

7. If the repayment of coupon and principal on a municipal bond depends on the success of the specific project funded by the bond, the bond is a _____ bond.

8. The _____ year Treasury bond provides the current benchmark risk-free rate.

9. Foreign bonds denominated in British pound sterling and sold in Great Britain are called _____ bonds.

10. Foreign bonds denominated in _____ and sold in Japan are called Samurai bonds.

ESSAY QUESTIONS

1. Do Treasury bonds require an indenture?

2. Why do investors like corporate bonds to have sinking funds, but investors do not like call provisions? Recall that sinking fund provisions are occasionally met by a random call of a portion of the outstanding bonds.

3. Why don't investors simply purchase those bonds that offer the highest returns? Isn't that the objective, to maximize your wealth?

4. Are default free, zero coupon Treasury STRIPS low risk or high risk? Distinguish between the risk that the price of the bond will change when interest rates change and the risk involved in reinvesting the cash flows of an investment as interest rates change.

INTERNET EXERCISES

1. Try Bonds Online - http://www.bondsonline.com - for a comprehensive treatment of bond quotes, news, etc. This busy Web site has a lot of links you can try. Under "General Information," try the "What kind of investor are you?" link. So, what kind of investor are you?

2. Another comprehensive site relating to bonds is http://www.finpipe.com/fixed.htm - which is the Web site for Financial Pipeline's coverage of bonds. Click on "Types of Bonds" and extend your knowledge.

The Stock Market

SUMMARY

1. Stocks (equities) represent ownership of a corporation. Traditional preferred stock pays a fixed dividend while the dividend on common stock varies. Preferred stock is preferred in that (a) usually the corporation cannot pay a common dividend until it pays its preferred dividend, including all past preferred dividends it failed to pay and (b) in the event of liquidation, preferred shareholders have a priority claim, up to the par value of the preferred stock, over the claims of common shareholders. Common shareholders have the right to vote their shares to elect the corporation's board of directors and to vote on other matters that may be on the agenda of the annual meeting.

2. Equity represents a significant source of funding for DSUs and the efficient allocation of capital to deserving enterprises is the equity markets most important economic function. Disruptions of the equity market harm this allocation function and are of concern to economists, investors, and policy makers. Markets that overreact to positive and/or negative news and markets susceptible to "speculative bubbles" are of concern. Speculative bubbles occur when stock prices are bid up to unsustainably high levels. The subsequent crash as the bubble bursts is capable of inflicting long-term harm on the economy (e.g., Japan during the 1990s).

3. Stocks are issued in the primary market generally with the assistance of investment bankers (underwriters). An initial public offering (IPO) is the very first time stocks are issued to the public. IPOs are often quite volatile, allowing for some spectacular gains, but also the possibility of tremendous losses. Stocks subsequently trade in the secondary market through either exchange trading or in the over-the-counter market. Organized exchanges, such as the New York Stock Exchange (NYSE), use the specialist system to trade stocks. Customers send their orders to brokerage houses that own seats on the exchange. The broker takes the order to the specialist post and offers to buy or sell (as appropriate) from or to other exchange members. If no other members are willing to trade, the specialist will always execute the trade out of his or her inventory. Computer advances (i.e., the designated order turnaround, or DOT, system) now allow many trades to be directed directly to the specialist. Each stock traded on the exchange is assigned to one, and only one, specialist. In contrast, over-the-counter (OTC) trading involves multiple market makers. The most important OTC market is the NASDAQ market. The NASDAQ computer/telephone system connects the many market makers that trade OTC stocks and allows for rapid transmittal of bid and ask prices. To execute an order, one's agent (stockbroker) calls one of the dealers who "makes a market" in that stock and negotiates to buy or sell the stock with that dealer. To make a market is to state publicly that you stand ready to buy or sell from or to the public. The debate as to whether the single market maker system on the exchanges or the multiple market maker system used by NASDAQ results in more efficient trading (e.g., smaller bid ask spreads) remains an active debate.

4. Equity investments, in general, carry more risk than does investing in bonds. For one thing, dividends are more uncertain than coupon and maturity payments. Furthermore, stocks tend to exhibit greater price (and return) volatility than bonds. That is, stock prices are more changeable. If for some unfortunate reason one must sell stocks during a period when their prices are low, one might suffer significant losses. Because of their risk, stocks generally have higher expected returns (but remember, expectations don't always come true). These high expected returns make stocks very attractive investment for investors with relatively long-term horizons. One of the more spectacular examples of market risk is the 22% drop in equity prices on October 19, 1987. One response to the crash was the creation of "circuit breakers" that are designed to interrupt trading if conditions suggest that the market is overreacting. The basic scheme of the current circuit breakers, ignoring the more intricate rules, are: a one-hour halt in trading if the Dow Jones Industrial Average falls by 10%, a two-hour halt if the Dow falls by 20%, and if the Dow falls by 30%, the market closes for the day.

4. Margin trading allows investors to leverage the potential returns on their investments. Although investors can buy bonds and T-bills on margin, margin trading is generally approached from an equity perspective. Equity investors can borrow up to 50% of the value of the stocks they purchase. Thus, if you had $5,000, you could borrow another $5,000 from your stockbroker and purchase $10,000 worth of stock. If you're right and the stocks increase in value, your rate of return will be, loosely speaking, twice the rate of return you otherwise would have. However, if you're wrong, you'll see your money disappearing twice as fast as it otherwise would. Margin loans are relatively low risk loans for brokerage houses to make, as the house will hold the shares in the margin account as collateral. But if prices fall enough, the broker will begin to worry that the shares now represent insufficient collateral against the loan. At that point, the broker will demand that the investor post additional cash as additional collateral against the loan. This is a margin call. To calculate when such a margin call will occur, divide the loan amount by one minus the maintenance margin percentage. Thus, to continue our example, if the maintenance margin on our $10,000 margin account with a $5,000 loan is 30%, divide $5,000 by 0.7; the investor will receive a margin call when the value of the investment falls below $7,142.86. If you can't post the cash required by a margin call, your broker will sell the stock, pay off the loan, and return any remaining funds to you.

5. Equity mutual funds pool the funds of many investors and purchase shares in hundreds of companies. Small investors thus achieve diversification, which reduces the risk associated with holding only a small number of equity issues, and also have professional managers selecting and monitoring their portfolio.

6. Stock market indexes are used to gauge the general tone of the market and to provide a benchmark against which one can measure his or her portfolio's performance. The best-known index is the Dow Jones Industrial Average of 30 large (but not necessarily the largest) stocks in the country. The Dow is a price-weighted index. Component stocks with higher prices per share have a greater impact on the Dow, even though they might not be as important to the economy. Furthermore, price weighted indexes must adjust the divisor used in the index when stocks are added or removed from the index or when stocks "split" their shares. The divisor for the Dow is not thirty. Over the years, the divisor for the Dow has fallen and in late 2001 it was below 0.15. When you divide by a number less than one, you actually multiply the value of the numerator. This explains why the point moves of the Dow are so much greater than they used to be. The sum of the thirty prices is effectively being multiplied by almost seven instead of being divided by thirty. Most other indexes are value weighted, where value is defined to be the price per share times the number of shares outstanding. Value weighting avoids most of the distortions caused by price weighting.

7. The value of a stock, in theory, is the present value of the cash flows associated with the stock (i.e., its dividends) discounted back to present value at an appropriate discount rate. Dividends are difficult to estimate. Furthermore, stocks do not "mature" as bonds do; stocks exist, in theory, forever. Given the risky characteristics stocks possess, finding the right discount rate to use is also a difficult task. We can simplify the process by assuming that dividends grow at a constant rate forever and that the discount rate is greater than that growth rate. Under such conditions, the current price of the stock, P_0, is a function of the current dividend, D_0, the growth rate, g, and the discount rate, d. Algebraically:

$$P_0 = D_0 (1 + g) / (d - g)$$

8. To estimate the discount rate, d, we can use the capital asset pricing model (CAPM) and estimates of the risk-free rate, R_f, the market rate, R_m, and the stock's beta, b (a measure of the risk of the stock relative to the risk of the entire stock market). Note the text, in formula 11-3, uses the symbol R_m to be the market risk premium. A risk premium is the asset's return in excess of the risk-free return. I think the following expression of the CAPM is more clear:

$$d = R_f + b (R_m - R_f)$$

9. Corporations can finance operations or expansion through either internal financing or external financing. Internal financing means reinvesting the cash flows earned by the company into the company. External financing means issuing either new debt or new equity. Using more debt creates more leverage. Leverage can increase returns on the equity invested in the company when the company earns more than the interest cost of the debt, but using more debt increases the risk of bankruptcy. This particular risk-return trade off is one of the most challenging questions in finance and has generated a large amount of research. Capital structure decisions remain, nonetheless, mostly a matter of managerial judgment rather than clear economic answers.

TRUE/FALSE QUESTIONS

T F 1. Stocks trade either on the primary market represented by the New York Stock Exchange and the other exchanges or on the secondary markets such as the OTC market and the NASDAQ.

T F 2. Traditional preferred stock pays a fixed dividend, while the dividend on a share of common stock might vary and could even fall to zero.

T F 3. The secondary market for stocks can be divided into two major categories – exchange trading and over-the-counter trading.

T F 4. Companies with many exceptionally attractive growth opportunities will likely have little need for external financing, all else held equal.

T F 5. Mutual funds allow small investors to gain the advantages of diversification and professional management of their portfolio decisions.

Chapter 11 — The Stock Market

T F 6. Buying stocks on margin provides investors with the ability to reduce the risks of owning stocks at a cost of reducing the returns available on the portfolio due to the interest that must be paid on the margin loan.

T F 7. Over long-term horizons, the rate of return on bonds generally outperforms that on stocks.

T F 8. There are more than twice as many mutual funds in existence than the number of stocks that trade actively on the NYSE.

T F 9. The Dow Jones Industrial Average is a value-weighted index of 500 stocks.

T F 10. Value-weighted stock indexes do not need to adjust the divisor used in their calculations because of stock splits; price-weighted indexes do need to make such adjustments.

T F 11. Beta is a measure of systematic risk. It captures the relative sensitivity of the returns on a stock to the returns on the entire stock market.

T F 12. A stock with a growth rate higher than its required rate of return would sell for a negative price.

T F 13. The U.S. stock market declined dramatically in the middle of October 1987. The Japanese stock market fell by more than 50% in the early 1990s. These market crashes had roughly equivalent impact on their respective national economies.

T F 14. A corporate "raider" intent on a hostile takeover of a target corporation would try to buy a sufficient number of shares of preferred shares so as to be able to elect a majority of the members of the board of directors.

T F 15. If the market return is expected to be 9.5% and the beta of a stock with an expected return of 7.875 is 0.75, the risk-free rate of return is 5%.

T F 16. Companies that fail to pay the expected dividend on their common stock are said to be in "equity default.:

T F 17. Diversification is most effective when there is perfect positive correlation between the returns of the stocks held in the portfolio.

T F 18. The NYSE and the NASDAQ system are both elements of the secondary market in stocks.

T F 19. If the Dow rises by 10% above its threshold level and it is not yet 2:00 p.m. in New York, trading on the exchange will be stopped for one hour.

T F 20. Program trading involves the buying and selling of a set of securities (a program of trades) as if they were one security.

T F 21. Wall Street is so named because it is the site of the wall built by the Dutch to separate the settlement of New Amsterdam from the rest of Manhattan.

T F 22. There are 5,000 stocks in the Wilshire 5,000 Index.

Chapter 11   The Stock Market

T F   23.   October, this is one of the peculiarly dangerous months to speculate in stocks. The others are July, January, September, April, November, May, March, June, December, August, and February. (Mark Twain)

MULTIPLE CHOICE QUESTIONS

1. A stock has a beta of 1.25. If the risk-free rate is 4% and the expected return on the market is 12%, the rate of return on the stock that is consistent with the CAPM, is:
   a. 20.0%
   b. 16.0%
   c. 14.0%
   d. 12.5%

2. Assume you invest $5,000 into a portfolio of stocks and leave the money in the account for the next forty years. If the stocks pay an average return of 14% annually, what will be the value of the account at the end of the forty years? (Hint: raise 1.14 to the 40th power)
   a. more than $1,000,000
   b. more than $900,000, but less than $1,000,000
   c. more than $500,000 but less than $900,000
   d. less than $500,000

3. Assume you invest $5,000 into a portfolio of bonds and leave the money in the account for the next forty years. If the bonds pay an average return of 7% annually, what will be the value of the account at the end of the forty years? (Hint: raise 1.07 to the 40th power)
   a. more than $500,000
   b. more than $250,000, but less than $500,000
   c. more than $100,000 but less than $250,000
   d. less than $100,000

4. Refer to your answers to questions 2 and 3 above. If the rate of return your neighbor earns on her $5,000 single deposit retirement account is 7% and the rate of return you earn on your $5,000 single deposit retirement account is twice as high at 14%, after a 40 year working life (choose the one best answer):
   a. you will have more than ten times the money available at retirement than will your neighbor
   b. you will have more than twice the money available at retirement as your neighbor
   c. you will have twice the money available at retirement as your neighbor
   d. you will have the same amount of money at retirement as your neighbor

5. You borrow $4,000 from your broker and put up $6,000 of your own money to buy $10,000 worth of stock on margin. If the maintenance margin requirement is 30%, you will get a margin call when the value of the stock touches:
   a. $8,571.43
   b. $6,000.00
   c. $5,714.29
   d. $4,000.00

6. A stock pays a current dividend of $3.00. Dividends are expected to grow at 5% for the foreseeable future. If the risk-free rate is 3%, the expected market return is 11%, and the stock has a beta of 0.95, calculate the price of the stock using the discounted dividend model.
   a. $56.25
   b. $30.00
   c. $27.75
   d. $ 3.15

7. The most often used term to refer to occasions when the prices of stocks appear to be driven to irrationally high levels amidst a general sense of euphoria is:
   a. euphoric market
   b. speculative bubble
   c. irrational exuberance
   d. triple witching hour

8. Which of the following terms is not associated with secondary market trading?
   a. underwriting
   b. NASDAQ
   c. NYSE
   d. program trading

9. If an investor with $55,000 cash wishes to fully margin a purchase of stock, how much stock would he be able to buy, given current initial margin requirements?
   a. $155,000
   b. $110,000
   c. $ 86,667
   d. $ 55,000

10. Stocks with betas above one:
    a. are more volatile than the stock market as a whole
    b. are less volatile than the market as a whole
    c. do not exist as beta cannot be greater than one
    d. move one-for-one with changes in the market as a whole

11. Who decides which stocks are included in the Dow Jones Industrial Average?
    a. Dow Jones & Company
    b. the Senate Select Committee on Stock Index Composition
    c. the Joint Congressional Committee on Securities Markets
    d. the President of the United States with the advice and consent of the Senate

12. A stock that is undervalued:
    a. should be bought
    b. should be sold
    c. cannot be purchased on margin
    d. none of the above

13. Different investors might have divergent opinions about the value of a stock because:
    a. they disagree on the stock's growth prospects
    b. they disagree on the stock's appropriate discount rate
    c. they disagree on general economic prospects
    d. all of the above

14. Price the following preferred stock. It pays a fixed dividend of $2.50 per share. The required rate of return on this stock is 8%. (Hint: since the dividend is fixed and never changes, what is the growth rate in dividends?)
    a. $40.00
    b. $31.25
    c. $20.00
    d. $16.67

15. All of the following are external financing except:
    a. issuing new preferred stock
    b. issuing new common stock
    c. issuing new long-term debt
    d. retaining current earnings

16. U.S. companies use more debt today, as a proportion of their assets, than they did twenty years ago. Why?
    a. debt is tax advantaged, equity is not
    b. leverage increases the rate of return companies earn on invested equity
    c. debt is less typically costly than equity (it requires a lower rate of return be paid to investors)
    d. all of the above
    e. none of the above

17. The New York Composite Index:
    a. is value-weighted
    b. consists of all stocks that trade on the NYSE
    c. contains industrial, transportation, utility, and financial stocks
    d. all of the above
    e. none of the above

FILL IN QUESTIONS

1. The divisor used in _____ indexes must be adjusted when component stocks split.

2. The largest stock exchange in the United States is the _____.

3. Trading halts designed to keep markets from overreacting to the downside are known as _____.

4. The oldest stock exchange in the United States is the _____. (Hint: think of Benjamin Franklin. Well then, think of Rocky Balboa)

5. Each stock traded on an exchange is assigned to one and only one market maker in that stock known as the _____.

6. The Dow Jones Industrial Average is _____ weighted.

7. The Standard & Poor's 500 is _____ weighted.

8. According to the discounted dividend model, stock prices are a function of _____, _____, and _____.

9. Bonds are debts owed by the corporation while equities represent _____ of the corporation.

10. The computer system that allows trades of 3,000 shares or less to be routed directly to the NYSE specialist is the _____ system.

ESSAY QUESTIONS

1. Mark Twain wrote that wives don't object to their husbands *gambling,* so much as to their husbands *losing.* What is it about speculative bubbles that draws more and more people into the market even as the prices grow more and more outrageous? Or is it that there's nothing wrong with the bubble, per se, we just need to find a way to keep such bubbles from ever bursting?

2. The Ford Motor Company was taken public in the mid-1950s. However, the proceeds of the issue went to the Ford Foundation, not to the company itself. Henry Ford had given thousands of shares of Ford Motor Company Stock to the foundation years before. People continue to speculate that the Ford family preferred to keep the company closely held and under family control. Assuming that is true, what could the Ford family have done to prevent the Ford Foundation from selling Ford Motor Company shares to the public?

3. In 1961, average daily volume on the NYSE was a bit more than 4 million shares a day. With approximately 220 trading days in a year, 1961 volume was around 880 million shares. Forty years later, on January 4, 2001, on that one trading day, NYSE trading was 2.129 billion shares. How is it possible that the NYSE now trades more shares in a single day than once were traded in an entire year?

INTERNET EXERCISES

1. The Philadelphia Stock Exchange Web site can be found at - http://www.phlx.com. Click on the "Products" link. What products does the PHLX feature? Why don't they feature equities like the NYSE? (Hint: what does the word "niche" mean).

2. Go to the NYSE Web site - http://www.nyse.com. Click on "The Trading Floor." Then click on "Anatomy of a Trade." Walk through the presentation. And now you know, and knowing is half the battle (Sorry about that. I guess I watched too many G.I. Joe cartoons with my kids when they were growing up!)

12

The Mortgage Market

SUMMARY

1. In recent years, mortgages, and instruments based on mortgages, have seen a substantial amount of innovation. These once staid, and rather unattractive, financial assets have been sliced and diced and repackaged and are now among the leading edge instruments of financial engineering. Financial engineering involves building for a client new financial assets with attractive characteristics by mixing the right combination of existing financial assets.

2. Mortgages are debts secured by real property. In the event of a default, the lender can repossess the property and sell it, with the proceeds used to pay off or pay down the loan. Most mortgages are amortized; the mortgage payment is sufficient to not only pay interest on the loan, but to reduce the balance owed on the loan. At the end of the term of the mortgage, the balance will be zero. The "closing costs" associated with mortgages can be significant. These costs include title insurance, origination fees, appraisals, surveys, recording fees and "points." A point is one percent of the loan. Three points on a $100,000 mortgage would be $3,000. Points are, in effect, pre-paid interest charges that reduce the stated interest rate of the loan. If you are willing to pay more points, the stated interest rate is lower, but the effective return to the lender remains competitive since you are just pre-paying some of the interest.

3. To qualify for a mortgage, borrowers must meet certain credit standards. The loan-to-value ratio is the amount of the mortgage applied for divided by the value of the property. Loan-to-value ratios that exceed 80% are given greater scrutiny by lenders. Such borrowers might be forced to purchase private mortgage insurance (PMI) to reduce default risk to the lender. In the event of default by the borrower, the PMI company will pay the lender. And then the PMI company will sue the borrower. This concern with loan-to-value ratios makes sense as it is far more likely that a borrower will default on a $100,000 property that has a $100,000 mortgage on it than if the property had only a $70,000 mortgage. In the first case, the borrower loses nothing, but in the second he or she loses $30,000. Lenders also look at the debt-to-income ratio of the borrower. Debt-to-income ratios relate monthly debt payments to monthly income. Debt-to-income ratios above 36% often lead to denial of the mortgage. In addition, the credit history of the borrower is reviewed, as the lender is interested in knowing if the borrower takes his or her obligations to repay loans seriously.

4. Mortgages may be either fixed or variable. On a fixed rate mortgage, the interest rate remains the same over the life of the mortgage. With variable rate or floating rate mortgages, the interest rises or falls in line with a reference interest rate such as the Treasury bill rate or the prime rates posted by major commercial banks. Most mortgages can be prepaid without penalty. Thus, when interest rates fall, many fixed rate mortgages are refinanced – the homeowner borrows money at the new lower interest rate and uses the money to pay off the older high rate mortgage. From the perspective of an

investor investing in mortgages, this prepayment feature is not attractive. From the investor's perspective, if interest rates go up, the value of the mortgage falls (as would be the case with any bond). However, if interest rates go down (sufficiently), the borrower pays off the mortgage and the investor (lender) must reinvest the proceeds at the new lower prevailing interest rate. Sort of a, "Heads, I win; tails, you lose" game. The U.S. federal government tried to make mortgages more attractive investments, and thus stimulate the housing sector, by sponsoring agencies that buy mortgages from banks, giving the banks more money that they can then use to make more mortgages. The agencies (Ginnie Mae, Fannie Mae, etc.) get the money to buy the mortgages by issuing bonds. These bonds are collateralized by pools of mortgages. In the case of Ginnie Mae (the Government National Mortgage Association), the bonds are guaranteed as to the timely payment of principal and interest by the U.S. federal government. Bonds issued by the other agencies have an "implicit" guarantee – most people believe that the federal government would not allow these agencies to default – but they are not formally guaranteed by the federal government.

5. The Federal Housing Administration and the Department of Veterans Affairs insure mortgage loans for borrowers that meet certain criteria. VA loans (for veterans) and FHA loans (for low-income borrowers) allow for low or zero down payments. The Government National Mortgage Association (Ginnie Mae), the Federal National Mortgage Association (Fannie Mae), and the Federal Home Loan Mortgage Corporation (Freddie Mac) are government-sponsored enterprises that, effectively, make a secondary market in mortgages. They issue bonds secured by pools of mortgages. Ginnie Mae bonds are "pass through" certificates. Ginnie Mae passes the coupon, principal, and prepayments of principal made on the pool of mortgages through to the bondholders. Bondholders are exposed to prepayment risk. Collateralized mortgage obligations (CMOs) are also backed by a pool of mortgages. CMOs repackage the cash flows from the pool in interesting ways. For example, they might slice the prepayments into several "tranches." The A tranche receives all prepayments up to a pre-specified amount; prepayments then flow to the B tranche, and then to the C tranche, etc. The A tranche is then a short-term instrument, the C tranche relatively long-term, and so on. These slices turn out to be more attractive to various investors than the mortgages themselves. By packaging the cash flows into attractive pieces, the sum of the values of the pieces exceeds the value of the whole.

6. Innovative mortgages include graduated payment mortgages that start out with low monthly payments that make it easier for borrowers to qualify; payments rise later in the life of the loan. Biweekly mortgages have 26 payments per year, a payment every two weeks. The principal on these mortgages is paid down faster than on monthly payment mortgages. Second mortgages are subordinate (lower priority of claim in event of default) mortgages made on the borrower's equity in the property.

7. Like other financial assets, the value of a mortgage is the present value of the cash flows of the mortgage. The proper interest rate to use to discount the cash flows depends on the term structure of interest rates and the risks of the mortgage. Mortgage valuation is further complicated by the possibility of prepayment. Calculating amortization schedules for mortgages can be done with financial calculators or computer spreadsheets. For financial calculators, first solve for the monthly payment of the mortgage. Then decide what months you want to see amortized and run the amortization function. For example, suppose we have a $120,000 mortgage for 30 years at a fixed rate of 8%. Using the HP 10BII, put 360 into N, 8/12 (i.e., 0.666666667) into i/yr, 120000 into PV, and 0 into FV. Then solve for payment (-880.52). If you want the first twelve months amortization, hit 1, then Enter, then 12, then 2nd function, then Amort. Cycle through the principal, interest and balance by repeatedly hitting the = key. Compare this procedure to the use of computer spreadsheet functions by completing essay question number 1 below.

Chapter 12 — The Mortgage Market

TRUE/FALSE QUESTIONS

T F   1. The rate of prepayments of principal on a pool of mortgages is difficult to predict; however, when interest rates fall, prepayments generally increase.

T F   2. The risk of default on mortgages is trivial, thus little effort is made by lenders to ascertain the credit risk of borrowers.

T F   3. Bonds issued by the Government National Mortgage Association (Ginnie Mae) are guaranteed by the federal government as to the timely payment of both interest and principal.

T F   4. The Federal Housing Administration (FHA) insures mortgages made by low-income borrowers.

T F   5. Most mortgages in the United States reflect amortization of the principal to a value of zero over the life of the loan.

T F   6. The bulk of mortgages in the U.S. are made against single-family residences.

T F   7. Adjustable rate mortgages (ARMs) reduce interest rate risk to the lender.

T F   8. As a guideline, mortgage lenders like the debt-to-income ratios of the borrower to be below 20 percent.

T F   9. Bonds issued by the Federal National Mortgage Association (Fannie Mae) are guaranteed by the federal government as to the timely payment of both interest and principal.

T F   10. Borrowers like the prepayment option, but mortgage lenders do not.

T F   11. A borrower is able to reduce the interest rate on a mortgage by paying points.

T F   12. Adjustable rate mortgages (ARMs) reduce default risk to the lender.

T F   13. As a guideline, mortgage lenders like the loan-to-value ratio of the property pledged against the loan to be 80 percent or less.

T F   14. A biweekly mortgage effectively makes 13 months of payments in a year.

T F   15. Bonds issued by the Federal Home Loan Mortgage Corporation (Freddie Mac) are guaranteed by the federal government as to the timely payment of both interest and principal.

T F   16. Graduated payment mortgages have lower payments in the early years of the mortgage thus making it easier for borrowers to qualify (i.e., have an acceptable debt-to-income ratio).

T F 17. In recent years, 70% of the homes sold in the United States were purchased with loans that were then packaged into pools securitizing bonds issued by Fannie Mae and Freddie Mac.

T F 18. If interest rates increase, the value of outstanding mortgages decrease.

T F 19. Holding other factors constant, if interest rates rise, the default risk on fixed rate mortgages increases more than the default risk on variable rate mortgages.

T F 20. The risk of default will increase if the value of the property pledged against the mortgage decreases.

T F 21. In the event of default, the property will be seized by the lender and sold in order to recover the loan. It should be noted that the balance owed on a first mortgage must be paid in entirety before any payment is made against a second mortgage.

MULTIPLE CHOICE QUESTIONS

1. Which, if any, of the following bonds are contractually guaranteed as to the timely payment of principal and interest by the federal government?
    a. Fannie Mae bonds
    b. Freddie Mac bonds
    c. Ginnie Mae bonds
    d. none of the above

2. As a guideline, to qualify for a mortgage, a borrower's debt-to-income ratio should not exceed:
    a. 80%
    b. 36%
    c. 20%
    d. 10%

3. As a guideline, to qualify for a mortgage without the need for private mortgage insurance, the loan-to-value ratio should not exceed:
    a. 80%
    b. 36%
    c. 20%
    d. 10%

4. As mortgages are amortized:
    a. most of the early payments reflect interest with little reduction in the balance owed
    b. principal is reduced at a constant rate over the life of the mortgage
    c. most of the early payments reflect reductions in the balance owed rather than interest
    d. interest is not charged on the loan until the loan is more than halfway to maturity

5. All of the following are insured by agencies of the federal government except:
   a. FHA mortgages
   b. conventional mortgages
   c. VA mortgages
   d. agencies of the federal government do not insure any mortgages

6. Default risk is higher if:
   a. the mortgage is for a longer term
   b. the down payment on the property is higher
   c. the loan-to-value ratio is higher
   d. both a and c

7. Which of the following statements is/are true regarding adjustable rate mortgages (ARMs)?
   a. ARMs show increased default risk when interest rates rise
   b. ARMs make it easier for borrowers to qualify for mortgages
   c. ARMs shift interest rate risk from the lender onto the borrower
   d. all of the above
   e. none of the above

8. Which of the following mortgages might exhibit negative amortization?
   a. graduated equity mortgages
   b. graduated payment mortgages
   c. fixed rate VA mortgages
   d. balloon mortgages

9. The minimum denomination for Ginnie Mae bonds is:
   a. $1,000,000
   b. $ 100,000
   c. $ 50,000
   d. $ 25,000

10. Ginnie Mae bonds have:
    a. no default risk
    b. no interest rate risk
    c. no prepayment risk
    d. all of the above

11. Ginnie Mae is a subsidiary of:
    a. Fannie Mae
    b. Freddie Mac
    c. HUD
    d. The U.S. Department of the Treasury

12. As of the year 2000, conforming loans have maximum values of:
    a. $325,666
    b. $252,700
    c. $135,650
    d. $127,500

13. The true maturity of a non-callable thirty year Treasury bond is _____ the true maturity of a thirty year conventional fixed rate mortgage which is carried to full term (i.e., is not prepaid).
    a. greater than
    b. equal to
    c. less than
    d. more information is needed to answer this question

14. The risk premium on a mortgage reflects:
    a. the potential for the borrower to default
    b. the low liquidity of mortgages in comparison to Treasury bonds
    c. the risk of receiving a repayment of principal early (i.e., prior to its expected repayment point)
    d. a and b
    e. all of the above

15. In considering whether or not to approve a mortgage, lenders look at:
    a. the borrower's debt-to-income ratio
    b. the loan-to-value ratio
    c. the borrower's credit history
    d. all of the above

16. U.S. companies use more debt today, as a proportion of their assets, than they did twenty years ago. Why?
    a. debt is tax advantaged, equity is not
    b. leverage increases the rate of return companies earn on invested equity
    c. debt is less typically costly than equity (it requires a lower rate of return be paid to investors)
    d. all of the above
    e. none of the above

17. Which of the following federal agencies guarantee mortgages?
    a. the Department of Veterans Affairs
    b. the Department of the Treasury
    c. the Department of Commerce
    d. the Department of the Interior
    e. none of the above

FILL IN QUESTIONS

1. If the initial payment in a graduated mortgage are not sufficient to cover the interest on the mortgage, the principal amount outstanding will _____, a condition known as _____ amortization.

2. The risk premium for uninsured mortgages is _____ that of insured mortgages.

3. In a strongly expanding economy, interest rates rise, _____ the risk of prepayment.

4. In a strongly expanding economy, default risk _____.

5. A _____ is a public record that stays with the property title and gives the mortgage lender the right to repossess the property if the borrower defaults.

6. The _____ ratio measures the monthly payments of the borrower relative to the borrower's monthly income.

7. The borrower's credit history is less important if there is a _____ down payment.

8. As a guideline, lenders are looking for borrowers to have debt-to-income ratios of _____ or less.

9. As a guideline, lenders are looking for mortgages to have loan-to-value ratios of _____ or less.

10. _____ is the term that describes having payments on a mortgage be sufficient to both pay interest on the outstanding balance and reduce the balance owed to zero at the end of the mortgage.

ESSAY QUESTIONS

1. Load up Excel on your computer. Use the CUMPRINC function to find the principal paid over the first twelve months of a $120,000 loan for thirty years, monthly payments, and an interest rate of 8%. Then use the CUMIPMT function to calculate the interest paid over the period. Do these values agree with those obtained by using your financial calculator (assuming you have a financial calculator)?

2. When mortgages are prepaid, investors that own the mortgages receive the principal earlier than they expected to receive it. Why is it bad to get your money back sooner than you expected to get it back?

INTERNET EXERCISES

1. Go to the Fannie Mae Web site - http://www.fanniemae.com - and click on "Mortgage-Backed Securities" under the "Investors" heading at the left margin of the page. Under "Product Data" on the left margin of the MBS page, click on "Latest Postings." Click on "SMBS Prospectuses." The prospectus will come up as an Adobe Acrobat file. Search the file for "risk factors" and repeat the search until you get to the page listing the risk factors to consider before investing in

these securities. Write down these risk factors. Give yourself plenty of paper, for the risk factors should continue for three to five pages of the prospectus.

2. Return to the introductory Web page for Fannie Mae - http://www.fanniemae.com. Click on "Stockholders" from the "Investors" menu at the left margin of the page. Click on "Monthly Disclosure of Interest Rate Risk, Credit Risk, Risk-Based Capital, and Liquidity, [Month, Day, Year]" near the bottom of the page. Is the effective duration gap for Fannie Mae mostly positive or generally negative? For more information about duration gap, see Chapter 21.

3. You can also investigate Mortgage Backed Securities at the Ginnie Mae Web site - http://www.ginniemae.gov. However, Ginnie Mae does not provide any investor information links. Why not?

13

The International Financial System

SUMMARY

1. Bretton Woods era – In 1944, finance ministers from the major industrialized nations of the world met at Bretton Woods, New Hampshire and designed a system of currency exchange that relied on the U.S. dollar as the world's official reserve currency. The dollar was pegged to gold at the rate of $35 per ounce of gold and the other currencies of the world were pegged to the dollar. In 1944, one pound sterling cost four U.S. dollars. Over the next few years, the supply of pounds relative to the supply of dollars in the foreign exchange market increased dramatically (equivalently, the demand for dollars increased relative to the demand for pounds). Think back to Chapter 8 and you can make some reasonable guesses as to why this happened. Under Bretton Woods, the Bank of England was expected to support the pound by buying pounds with dollars. However, it became more and more difficult for the Bank of England to acquire dollars with which they could buy pounds. Eventually, the BoE had to devalue the pound and establish a new fixed exchange rate between pounds and dollars more in line with economic conditions. By 1949, □1.00 = $2.80, a thirty percent decline in the value of the pound. Other such currency problems existed under Bretton Woods. If a country's currency weakened against the dollar, it was expected to sell dollars and buy its currency. If a country's currency strengthened against the dollar, the country would sell dollars to the U.S. in exchange for gold. When the dollar itself weakened considerably in the early 1970s, the U.S. was forced to devalue by resetting the price of gold to $42 per ounce. By 1973, the U.S. simply refused to redeem dollars for gold, effectively destroying the currency exchange regimen of the Bretton Woods Accord. However, the International Monetary Fund (IMF) and the World Bank, which were formed at Bretton Woods, remain.

2. Floating exchange rates era – The Jamaica Agreement of 1974 officially adopted floating exchange rates. Under floating exchange rates, exchange rates are determined by supply and demand in the currency exchange marketplace. Risk management tools such as currency forwards and currency options were developed in response to the day-to-day fluctuations in exchange rates. The U.S. dollar remains the most important reserve currency held by banks, but the Japanese yen and the new Euro are also important parts of international bank reserves.

3. The Bank for International Settlements (BIS) predates Bretton Woods, having been created in 1930. The BIS acts as a bank for central banks. The central banks of some 120 countries have deposits with the BIS. The BIS acts as a trustee (overseer) for international financial agreements and has helped to standardize international financial practices. Forty-nine countries are members of the BIS. The bank's board of directors includes the central banks of eleven nations including the U.S., Japan, the U.K., France, and Germany.

4. The International Monetary Fund (IMF) was established at Bretton Woods. Nations experiencing balance of payment problems ask the IMF for loans to help them through the crisis. Borrowers must agree to abide by financial constraints imposed by the IMF in order to receive these loans. These conditions are often unpopular and would not have been adopted absent IMF pressure. The IMF created special drawing rights (SDRs), which are bookkeeping entries that reflect a weighted average of the values of the U.S dollar, the euro, the yen, and the pound sterling. Central banks settle transactions between each other using SDRs.

5. The World Bank was also established at Bretton Woods. The World Bank is an investment bank that issues bonds and uses the proceeds to make loans primarily to the governments of poor countries. The International Bank for Reconstruction and Development and the International Development Association are the operating subsidiaries of the World Bank. The International Finance Corporation is legally separate from the World Bank, but acts in association with the World Bank to channel investment funds to private enterprises in poor countries.

6. Suppose you could borrow in Japan for one year at 1% interest and that you could invest that money in the U.S. for one year at 6% interest. For the purposes of this simple little story let's assume that both loans are risk-free. Would you be able to make a nice profit without investing any of your own money? Such a zero-risk, zero-investment profit is called an arbitrage profit. However, note that the exchange rate between dollars and yen might change. Given today's exchange rate, there is an expected exchange rate one year from today that will just eliminate this arbitrage. This point, where the arbitrage is just eliminated, describes interest rate parity. To continue our above example, if the current yen-dollar exchange rate is 120 yen equals one dollar, interest rate parity holds if the expected yen-dollar exchange rate in one year is 114.34. Work it out. If you borrow 120 yen, then in one year you will owe 121.20 yen (at 1% interest). Invest the $1.00 you get by exchanging your yen for dollars at today's rate and in one year you will have $1.06 (at 6% interest). To avoid arbitrage, when you translate your $1.06 back into yen, it must equal 121.20 yen, an exchange rate of 114.34. It is worth noting that if interest rate parity holds, the real rate of return will be equal for the two nations.

TRUE/FALSE QUESTIONS

T F   1. Under the Bretton Woods Accord, the role of the U.S. central bank was, essentially, to sell gold to those central banks that wished to exchange dollars for gold and to buy gold for dollars from those central banks that wished to acquire more dollars.

T F   2. Under the Bretton Woods Accord, central banks that no longer could acquire dollars to support their currencies at the established rate would eventually have to devalue their currencies.

T F   3. Under the gold standard, such as during the Bretton Woods era, it was not possible for the United States to experience inflation.

T F   4. Under a fixed exchange rate system, currencies are not allowed to fluctuate day-to-day in response to changes in supply and/or demand.

Chapter 13   The International Financial System

T F   5. The International Monetary Fund (IMF) makes loans to poor nations directed towards the development of the infrastructure of those nations.

T F   6. Under floating exchange rates, if the U.S. balance of payments grows larger, holding all else constant, the U.S. dollar is likely to fall in value relative to most world currencies.

T F   7. The IMF is a subsidiary of the United Nations.

T F   8. The World Bank is a subsidiary of the United Nations.

T F   9. The Bank for International Settlements (BIS) is a subsidiary of the United Nations.

T F   10. Special drawing rights (SDRs) are used to settle transactions among the world's leading central banks.

T F   11. A private corporation in Guinea-Bissau would be more likely to seek a loan from the International Finance Corporation than from the World Bank.

T F   12. Oddly enough, the United States is not a member of the Bank for International Settlements (BIS).

T F   13. Bonds issued by the World Bank usually cannot achieve an investment grade rating and are, therefore, part of the "junk" bond market.

T F   14. During the Asian currency crisis of 1997, the IMF extended loans to several Asian nations, but forced those nations to adopt expansionary economic policies that they would not otherwise have adopted.

T F   15. Under floating exchange rates, central bank interventions into currency markets have been reduced in number.

T F   16. Under floating exchange rates, no nation any longer ties its currency to the U.S. dollar at a fixed rate.

T F   17. The official currency of the Republic of Panama is the U.S. dollar.

T F   18. The official currency of the United States of Mexico is the U.S. dollar.

T F   19. Currency exchange risk can be hedged using foreign exchange forward contracts.

T F   20. By returning to the gold standard, the United States could ensure that it would never again encounter a deficit in its balance of payments.

T F   21. If interest rate parity holds, the real rates of return for the countries will be equal.

MULTIPLE CHOICE QUESTIONS

1. A nation running an increasing balance of payments deficit is likely to see its currency:
   a. increase in value
   b. decrease in value
   c. replaced by special drawing rights (SDRs)
   d. management policies fall under the direction of the IMF

2. The nation of Xenon has seen it currency move from 120 xenas equals $1.00 to 145 xenas equals $1.00. The xena has:
   a. lost value relative to the value
   b. increased in value relative to the dollar
   c. the relative value of the xena to the dollar can not be determined unless we know both the Xenon inflation rate and the United States inflation rate
   d. there is no nation called Xenon so how can I be expected to answer this question

3. If gold were to rise from $280 per ounce to $325 per ounce:
   a. gold has appreciated against the dollar
   b. the dollar is weaker relative to gold
   c. it will not necessarily change the dollar yen exchange rate
   d. all of the above
   e. none of the above

4. Under floating exchange rates, which of the following **directly** impact the pound sterling – Japanese yen exchange rate?
   a. supply of U.S. dollars per month
   b. demand for U.S. dollars per month
   c. U.S. domestic incomes
   d. all of the above
   e. none of the above

5. Which of the following currencies are considered major reserve currencies?
   a. Japanese yen
   b. British pound sterling
   c. the Euro
   d. all of the above
   e. none of the above

6. Which of the following organizations makes loans to nations experiencing balance of payments difficulties?
   a. the World Bank
   b. the International Monetary Fund
   c. the Bank for International Settlements
   d. the United Nations
   e. none of the above

Chapter 13   The International Financial System

7. Which of the following organizations makes loans to private enterprises in developing nations?
   a. the World Bank
   b. the International Finance Corporation
   c. the Private Enterprise Development Corporation
   d. the United Nations
   e. none of the above

8. Which of the following organizations makes loans to fund public projects in poor countries, including projects such as roads, bridges, and sewers?
   a. the World Bank
   b. the International Monetary Fund
   c. the Bank for International Settlements
   d. the United Nations
   e. none of the above

9. Which of the following organizations makes loans to wealthy nations to assist with infrastructure projects?
   a. the World Bank
   b. the International Monetary Fund
   c. the Bank for International Settlements
   d. the United Nations
   e. none of the above

10. Special drawing rights (SDRs):
    a. are convertible into U.S. dollars at a fixed rated
    b. are backed by the gold reserves of the IMF
    c. reflect a weighted average value of the dollar, yen, euro, and pound sterling
    d. none of the above

11. Which of the following enterprises was not created by the Bretton Woods Accord?:
    a. the World Bank
    b. the International Monetary Fund
    c. the Bank for International Settlements
    d. all of the above were formed by the Bretton Woods Accord
    e. none of the above were formed by the Bretton Woods Accord

12. Which of the following do not belong to the "Group of Seven" (the G-7) countries:
    a. Russia
    b. China
    c. India
    d. none of the above are members of the G-7 countries
    e. all of the above are members of the G-7 countries

13. The Bank for International Settlements:
    a. facilitates trading of currency forwards and currency options
    b. monitors financial aspects of U.N. peacekeeping forces
    c. subsidizes U.S. exports
    d. is basically a bank for central bankers

14. With the fall of the Bretton Woods Accord:
    a. the U.S. dollar lost its value as a reserve currency
    b. the value of the U.S. dollar was no longer fixed in terms of gold
    c. the pound sterling became the sole major world currency whose price is fixed relative to silver
    d. the era of floating exchange rates came to an end
    e. b and d

15. All of the following organizations are headquartered in Washington, D.C. except:
    a. the International Monetary Fund
    b. the Bank for International Settlements
    c. the World Bank
    d. none of the above are headquartered in Washington, D.C.

16. Bretton Woods is located in:
    a. California
    b. Washington, D.C.
    c. New York
    d. New Hampshire

17. Assume interest rate parity holds. If the one-year U.S. risk-free rate is 5.5% and the one-year, risk-free rate in Germany is 7.5%, given that the current exchange rate between dollars and deutschmarks is 2.2 marks equals one dollar, the expected exchange rate in one year must be:
    a. 2.15907 marks to the dollar
    b. 2.20000 marks to the dollar
    c. 2.24171 marks to the dollar
    d. 2.24400 marks to the dollar

18. Assume interest rate parity holds. You know that today's exchange rate between the U.S. dollar and the Irish punt is that one dollar equals 0.88 punts. Let us assume that you also know that the exchange rate one year from today will be one dollar equals 0.95 punts. If the one-year, risk-free interest rate in Ireland is 12%, the one-year, risk-free interest rate in the U.S. must be:
    a. 42.862%
    b. 3.747%
    c. 1.000%
    d. −4.441%

FILL IN QUESTIONS

1. The _____ makes loans to assist poor nations develop public projects.

2. The International Bank for Reconstruction and Development is a subsidiary of the _____.

3. In general, the remedies imposed by the IMF on nations seeking loans are that the borrowers must pursue _____ fiscal policies designed to _____ consumption.

4. Nations whose balance of payments is seriously in deficit might seek assistance from _____.

5. If _____ holds then real rates of returns in the two countries are equal.

6. The bank for central bankers is the _____.

7. Over the years, the membership fees (quotas) and the pro-rata voting rights that the U.S. has in the IMF have _____.

8. If interest rates are higher in one nation than in another, and if interest rate parity holds, then the nation with the higher interest rates is expected to see its currency _____ relative to the lower interest rates nation.

9. The system of fixed exchange rates in effect from 1944 through 1973 was established by the _____.

10. The Bank for International Settlements is headquartered in _____.

ESSAY QUESTIONS

1. Try to think of some safeguards that you might impose on the World Bank to increase the likelihood that World Bank loans to developing nations are actually used to build the projects they are directed at. Is it important that such safeguards exist?

2. List several reasons why interest rate parity might not hold in the real world.

3. Consider the typical IMF remedy for nations experiencing balance of payments problems. Would it make sense for a nation barely above the economic subsistence level to adopt these IMF prescriptions? What other choices might they have?

INTERNET EXERCISES

1. The World Bank Web site - http://www.worldbank.org - has links to the International Bank for Reconstruction and Development, the International Development Association, and the International Finance Corporation, among other links. Check out the latest news for the IBRD, the IDA, and the IFC. Look at each organization's latest annual report. Which nations received the most assistance last year?

2. Is there more to the IMF than being the tough taskmaster to nations with balance of payments problems? Find out at - http://www.imf.org.

14

An Introduction to Financial Intermediaries and Risk

SUMMARY

1. Financial intermediaries (FIs) are involved in indirect finance. Recall that in direct finance, SSUs invest money directly with DSUs and generate a direct claim on the DSU. In indirect finance, SSUs invest with financial intermediaries such as banks, insurance companies, and pension companies. The SSUs have a claim on the bank, or on the insurance company, etc. The banks and insurance companies, etc., in turn invest into the SSUs. Use of specialized intermediaries to connect SSUs to DSUs greatly increases the effectiveness of financial markets. Financial intermediaries are experts at analyzing investment opportunities, they monitor the performance of the DSUs, they allow SSUs to hold diversified portfolios, and they greatly reduce default and other risks faced by SSUs.

2. Financial intermediaries are highly regulated. Financial intermediaries must deal with the potential for default by the DSUs. Changes in interest rates greatly affect the value of FIs. A run on the deposits of a FI may drain liquidity from the FI and cause it to fail. Risks presented by the increased internationalization of finance also impact FIs, especially exchange rate risk. In short, FIs are heavily regulated because they face serious risks and should an FI fail it might harm a large number of SSUs.

3. Various classifications of FIs can be generated. One is to group FIs that accept deposits (banks, saving association, and credit unions) separately from FIs that do not accept deposits, per se, but instead issue contracts (insurance companies and pension funds). Other FIs are involved in investment products (mutual funds) and finance company operations.

4. Depository institutions (banks, savings associations, and credit unions) acquire funds through checking accounts, savings accounts, and time deposits (nonnegotiable CDs). Some might also issue bonds, borrow fed funds, borrow using repos, or borrow in non-U.S. markets. These institutions use the funds so acquired to make loans, including commercial loans, mortgage loans, consumer loans, and they also buy government and municipal securities.

5. Contractual-type intermediaries sell contracts, usually for a recurrent payment called a premium, that allow the purchasers of the contracts to make claims against the FI should certain contingencies arise. For example, you buy car insurance. You pay a quarterly premium for the insurance. If you have an accident, the insurance company agrees to pay all or a portion of the costs associated with the accident. Investment companies pool savings from thousands of SSUs and purchase a diversified set of securities. They provide a vehicle allowing small SSUs to invest into securities markets. Finance companies make loans against consumer durables (washer, refrigerators, etc) and also finance inventory and accounts receivable for small businesses.

6. The United States and most nations in the world operate under fractional reserve banking systems. When banks acquire deposits they must place some portion of the deposits on reserve. By buying or selling T-bills through open market activities, the Federal Reserve changes the amount of reserves available to the banking system. If the Fed makes more reserves available, banks will be able to make more new loans. These new loans, in turn, generate more deposits into the system, which allows more loans to be made, which generates even more deposits, and then there even more loans, and so on. Thus, a relatively small increase in reserves will generate multiple increases in deposits and loans. This is the money multiplier discussed in the Appendix to Chapter 14. The simplest estimate of the value of this multiplier is the inverse of the required reserve ratio. Thus, if the required reserve ratio is 5%, the multiplier is 20. If the required reserve ratio is 10%, the multiplier is 10. A more sophisticated money multiplier estimate can be found by taking into account the fact that banks often hold excess reserves, that banks desire to hold excess reserves in part depends on monetary changes, and the additional fact that the public adjusts its desired currency-to-deposits ratio as monetary conditions fluctuate. This more complex multiplier is:

$$\Delta M = \Delta MB \left[(1 + c) / (r_D + e + c) \right]$$

where ΔM is the change in the money supply, ΔMB is the change in the monetary base (the monetary base equals total reserves in the banking system plus currency in the hands of the public), c represents the desired currency-to-deposits ratio of the public, r_D is the required reserve ratio for deposits, and e represents the excess reserve percentage. Suppose that $c = 0.25$, $e = 0.02$, and $r_D = 0.03$. The money multiplier would then be: $[1.25 / (0.03 + 0.02 + 0.25)] = 4.1667$. What would the simple money multiplier be? The answer is 33.3333.

TRUE/FALSE QUESTIONS

T F 1. Under a fractional reserve banking system, only a portion of the deposits banks acquire can be lent out or otherwise invested into private commercial enterprise. T

T F 2. If interest rates increase on deposits faster than do the rates of return on loans and other bank investments, bank profitability will fall, and may even become negative. T

T F 3. A bank run occurs when the value of the bank's common stock increases several days in a row (the stock is said to have "run up"). F

T F 4. Checking deposits and savings deposits are liabilities to a bank. T

T F 5. Growth in credit union deposits has been phenomenal over the past twenty years. The largest credit unions now rival the large money center banks of New York in the size of their deposit base. F

T F 6. Historically, claims against property and casualty insurers have been far less predictable from year to year than claims made against life insurance companies. T

T F 7. Commercial banks pay federal income taxes, but most credit unions are tax-exempt. T

T F 8. Pension funds do not pay federal income taxes. T

T F 9. Pension funds have a greater need for liquidity than property and casualty insurance companies have. **F**

T F 10. Loans made by savings associations (S&Ls and savings banks) are primarily mortgages. **T**

T F 11. Money market mutual funds invest primarily in short-term, highly liquid instruments such as T-bills and commercial paper. **T**

T F 12. Pension fund financial assets now exceed the financial assets of commercial banks. **T**

T F 13. If the required reserve ratio for deposits is increased from 3% to 4%, holding all other factors constant, the money multiplier will also increase. **F**

T F 14. Given the deregulation of the financial system over the past ten years, opening a bank today is as simple as placing a sign in front of a storefront and inviting people in to make deposits. **F**

T F 15. Given the deregulation of the financial system over the past ten years, it is becoming more and more difficult to distinguish commercial banks from investment banks from insurance companies. **T**

T F 16. If a bank were to experience a serious run, they would turn to the Federal Reserve for assistance and borrow, on a temporary, emergency basis at the discount window. **T**

T F 17. Mortgages are assets to a savings and loan. **T**

T F 18. In excess of 98% of commercial bank assets are financed with debt. **T**

T F 19. The monetary base consists of excess reserves plus currency in the hands of the public. **F**

T F 20. Currency held by commercial banks is not part of the monetary base. **F**

MULTIPLE CHOICE QUESTIONS

1. All of the following involve claims or potential claims against financial intermediaries except:
   a. checking accounts
   b. General Motors common stock
   c. pension fund account
   d. life insurance

   B

2. If the Federal Reserve supplies reserves to the banking system, and no other factors change, the simple money multiplier:
   a. will increase
   b. will not change
   c. will decrease
   d. more information is needed in order to answer this question

   B

3. If the required reserve on deposits is 4%, the simple money multiplier is:
   a. 25.00
   b. 4.00
   c. 0.25
   d. more information is needed in order to answer this question

   A

4. All of the following financial intermediaries accept deposits except:
   a. pension funds
   b. commercial banks
   c. credit unions
   d. savings banks

   A

5. All of the following pieces of legislation relate primarily to financial intermediaries except:
   a. the Financial Institutions Reform, Recovery, and Enforcement Act
   b. the Gramm-Leach-Bliley Act
   c. the Glass-Steagall Act
   d. the Taft-Hartley Act

   D

6. Assume that the required reserve ratio for deposits is 3.75%. If excess reserves in the banking system are 1.5% and the currency-to-deposits ratio for the public is 0.28, the money multiplier is:
   a. 26.6667
   b. 4.0000
   c. 3.8496
   d. 2.1111
   e. none of the above

   C

7. Which of the following would be considered "contractual-type" FIs?
   a. pension funds
   b. automotive finance companies
   c. credit unions
   d. commercial banks

   A

8. Which of the following services would you expect to find at a "financial supermarket?"
   a. checking accounts
   b. mutual funds
   c. life and property and casualty insurance
   d. all of the above
   e. none of the above

   D

9. A bank experiencing a run would turn to which of the following for help?
   a. the World Bank
   b. the Risk Management Emergency Response Corporation
   c. the Bank for International Settlements
   d. the Federal Reserve Bank in their district

   D

Chapter 14   An Introduction to Financial Intermediaries and Risk

10. Which of the following belong in the category "thrifts?"
    a. savings and loans
    b. credit unions
    c. savings banks
    d. all of the above
    e. none of the above

11. Which of the following terms refers primarily to checking accounts?
    a. savings deposits
    b. transactions deposits
    c. time deposits
    d. none of the above

12. A money market mutual fund would be likely to invest in which of the following securities?
    a. U.S Treasury bonds
    b. long-term municipal bonds
    c. perpetual, fixed income preferred stock
    d. commercial paper
    e. both a and d

13. A bank's spread is:
    a. the ranch, the ranch house, and the bunk house
    b. the number of common shares of the bank that trade in a typical trading day
    c. the interest rate(s) the bank earns on its assets minus the rate(s) it pays to acquire funds
    d. the difference between the bid price and the ask price on its stock

14. Of the following, the most predictable is:
    a. the number and intensity of hurricanes that will hit the Florida Gulf coast next year
    b. the damage from flooding in the upper Midwest next spring
    c. the percentage of 58 year old women who will die within one year
    d. the scores of the Duke vs. North Carolina basketball games this season

15. If total reserves are 100 and excess reserves are 4, then required reserves must be:
    a. 104
    b. 96
    c. 40
    d. none of the above

FILL IN QUESTIONS

1. When the Federal Reserve supplies reserves to the banking system, the effect on the money supply will be a _____ of the dollar amount of reserve the Fed supplies.

2. In the United States, banks can be chartered by either the _____ or by one of the _____.

3. Commercial banks are typically defined as institutions that both accept _____ and make _____.

4. _____ have a scheduled maturity, and if the funds are withdrawn before that date, there is a penalty (forfeiture of a portion of the interest earned).

5. In order to join a _____, one must share a "common bond" with the other members.

6. The effective tax rate on life insurance companies is typically _____ that which property and casualty insurers pay.

7. General Motors Acceptance Corporation (GMAC) would be classified as a _____ FI.

8. By law and regulation, commercial banks may not invest in _____.

9. A good example of the financial supermarket concept is _____, which is the nation's largest brokerage house, the second largest mutual fund company, the largest investment underwriter, and a major insurance broker.

10. Both _____ and _____ are FIs that are exempt from taxation.

ESSAY QUESTIONS and INTERNET EXERCISES

1. Try the Merrill Lynch Web site - http://www.ml.com. Click on the "Individual Investors" link. Need help with retirement planning or estate planning or investments? It's all there. Click on "Banking and Lending Services." ML has checking, savings, and credit cards. Click on "Estate Planning." Will ML sell you insurance?

2. Take a look at another financial superstore by going to the Citigroup Web site - http://www.citigroup.com. Click on the "lines of business" link. Which of the following businesses is Citigroup involved in: investments, banking, life insurance, casualty insurance, credit cards, or consumer finance?

15

Commercial Banking Structure, Regulation, and Performance

SUMMARY

1. Banking is certainly one of the most heavily regulated industries in the United States. Most of this regulation traces back to the Great Depression of the 1930s when many banks failed. The Glass-Steagall Act of 1933 put interest rate ceilings on the deposit accounts (the idea being to protect banks from paying "too much" to acquire funds), separated investment banking (underwriting) from commercial banking (a response to the real or perceived threat of excessive speculation on the part of commercial banks), and created the Federal Deposit Insurance Corporation (FDIC) to guarantee the safety of bank deposits and preclude bank runs. U.S. commercial banks are chartered by either the federal government (these national banks often have the word national or the letters NA for national association in their title) or by one of the states. Nationally chartered banks must belong to the Federal Reserve System and they must subscribe to the FDIC. State banks may join the Fed and/or the FDIC at their option. Almost all banks, national or state, choose FDIC insurance. Although numerous banks did fail in the 1980s, there was little panic among depositors because of their faith that the FDIC would make good their accounts (up to the maximums allowed by law). The FDIC is judged to one of the most successful government agencies in U.S. history.

2. The McFadden Act predates the Depression (it was passed in 1927). The act was designed to protect local banks from "predatory" acts by large banks. National banks were required to obey state laws regarding branches. Most states severely restricted the number of branches a bank could have. States wanted to avoid having only a few large banks with statewide branches; the states feared such concentration of financial power. Further justification was that by ensuring that a large number of banks existed, competition would bring about enhanced consumer service. The reality of the McFadden Act was that it created many local monopolies as large numbers of small towns were served solely by a single bank. Large banks could not branch into the small town because of the restrictions on branches. The McFadden Act was superseded by the Interstate Banking and Branching Efficiency Act of 1994. A strong trend to fewer but larger banks continues to operate in the U.S.

3. Banks have been able to expand geographically and offer a greater variety of financial services using the bank holding company structure. A bank holding company is a corporation with several subsidiaries, one of which is a commercial bank. Bank holding companies can enter into many businesses that the bank subsidiary itself cannot enter into. The Gramm-Leach-Bliley Act of 1999 allowed bank holding companies to convert to financial holding companies. Financial holding companies can enter into securities underwriting and dealing, insurance, virtually all financial

endeavors, and many non-financial businesses. The "financial superstores" mentioned in Chapter 14 are, by and large, financial holding companies.

4. The international component of banking in the U.S. has grown in importance. Foreign banks now own more than 15% of U.S. banking assets. Much of this internationalization has been driven by the advances in telecommunications. One can quite literally move billions of dollars around the world at the speed of light using electronic transfers. Banking is and will remain a highly competitive business that is international in scope.

5. The essence of bank management is making decisions about how to attract deposits (liabilities to the bank) and where to make investments (which loans to make and which financial assets to buy). The bank's balance sheet tells the story and much time is spent by both bank management and regulatory auditors in examining the balance sheet. The asset side of the balance sheet is of particular importance. In extending loans to corporations and individuals, banks face default risk, interest rate risk, liquidity risk, and exchange rate risk. Banks also face problems such as asymmetric information, where the borrower has better information than does the bank as to the true quality of a loan. Adverse selection arises when those who are most desperately in need of a loan work hardest to convince the bank to extend the loan, perhaps going so far as to fail to reveal important facts about their creditworthiness (hey, don't tell them about those three loans we closed yesterday or they won't give us this loan). Moral hazard exists when borrowers use funds for purposes other than the purpose given in the loan document (well, now that we have the money, I'll meet you at the racetrack at four). The 1990s were good years for bank profits as the spread between banks' cost of funds and banks' return on assets was large, allowing the industry to recover from the dismal 1980s.

TRUE/FALSE QUESTIONS

T F   1. The Glass-Steagall Act was passed prior to the Great Depression of the 1930s.

T F   2. The McFadden Act forced commercial banks to give up most securities underwriting activities.

T F   3. By restricting the number of branches any one bank could have, state banking laws succeeded in generating an environment of healthy competition based on a large number of relatively small banks.

T F   4. All nationally chartered commercial banks must belong to the Federal Reserve System.

T F   5. Given the relatively large number of bank failures in the 1980s, most observers have concluded that, while noble of purpose, the FDIC failed to achieve its regulatory goals.

T F   6. Citigroup, formed by merging Citicorp and Travelers Group, is a prime example of a bank holding company.

T F   7. Bank holding companies that become financial holding companies can underwrite initial public offerings of equities.

T F   8. Reserve requirements for state chartered banks are lower than those for nationally chartered banks.

Chapter 15   Commercial Banking Structure, Regulation, and Performance

T F   9. In Canada, a dozen large banks serve the needs of the entire nation, while in the United States more than 8,000 commercial banks still exist.

T F   10. Moral hazard refers to the tendency for those least creditworthy to work hardest to convince banks to extend loans to them.

T F   11. Generally speaking, it is reasonable to expect that the borrower has a better understanding of risks and potential return on a loan than does the lender.

T F   12. Bank deposits are guaranteed by the FDIC. Therefore, depositors do not spend time analyzing the riskiness of a bank's assets. This might allow the banks to take more risk than they otherwise would because even if these risky loans fail, depositors will not run to take their money out of FDIC insured accounts.

T F   13. A large proportion of bank liabilities are payable on demand.

T F   14. While banks can ill afford to ignore the level of interest rates, in general, banks are more concerned with the difference between the rates they must pay to attract deposits and the rates they earn on the loans they extend (i.e., the spread).

T F   15. While more than 8,000 commercial banks exist in the United States, the largest 82 banks, about one percent of the total number of banks, own about 70% of bank assets.

T F   16. Bank profitability declined sharply in the 1990s.

T F   17. While a bank can form a bank holding company and buy an insurance company, an insurance company cannot become a bank holding company by buying a bank.

T F   18. The Federal Reserve is the primary regulator of all bank holding companies.

T F   19. Nonbank financial intermediaries (credit unions, finance companies, etc.) have, in recent years, increased their share of the market for financial services.

T F   20. In combating the problem of adverse selection, banks have been accused, not always in jest, of only making loans to those applicants who can prove that they do not need the loan.

MULTIPLE CHOICE QUESTIONS

1. Which of the following businesses can a bank holding company engage in?
   a. real estate appraisal
   b. courier services
   c. insurance agency and underwriting
   d. a and b
   e. all of the above

2. Which of the following regulate at least a portion of banks in the U.S.?
   a. the Federal Reserve System
   b. the FDIC
   c. the Comptroller of the Currency
   d. a and c
   e. all of the above

3. Regulation Q:
   a. imposed ceilings on the interest rates that commercial banks could pay
   b. restricted the number of branches nationally chartered banks could have
   c. established the minimum capital requirements for bank holding companies
   d. guides the open market transaction of the FOMC

4. Which of the following pieces of legislation required nationally chartered banks to comply with the branching laws of the states they operated in?
   a. Glass-Steagall Act
   b. McFadden Act
   c. Gramm-Leach-Bliley Act
   d. Garn-St. Germain Act

5. Which of the following is/are chartered by the federal government?
   a. Dogpatch National Bank and Trust
   b. Bumstead Bank, NA
   c. Forty-seventh National Bank
   d. all of the above
   e. none of the above

6. In the comfortable, near-monopoly days prior to bank deregulation, the general rule for managing a bank was "3 – 6 – 3." The rule refers to:
   a. borrow at 3% (i.e., pay a passbook savings rate of 3%)
   b. lend at 6% (charge 6% interest on the loans you make)
   c. be on the first tee by three p.m.
   d. all of the above

7. Which of the following best describes expectations of change in the U.S. banking system:
   a. the importance of the Federal Reserve is declining
   b. there will be more, but smaller banks in the near future
   c. there will be fewer, but larger banks in the near future
   d. commercial banks will, for all practical purposes, cease to exist

8. Banks which make direct equity investments in non-financial businesses are best described as:
   a. foolhardy
   b. commercial banks
   c. merchant banks
   d. equity banks

Chapter 15 Commercial Banking Structure, Regulation, and Performance

9. Which of the following is/are chartered by one of the states?
   a. Utah National Bank
   b. Bank of Alabama NA
   c. National Bank of Kentucky
   d. all of the above
   e. none of the above

10. Commercial bank management requires decisions regarding each of the following except:
    a. types of deposits they will offer
    b. the interest rates they will charge on loans
    c. the types of loans they will make
    d. amount of reserves they are required to maintain

11. Which of the following federal offices charters national banks?
    a. Comptroller of the Currency
    b. Board of Governors of the Federal Reserve System
    c. Federal Deposit Insurance Corporation
    d. Federal Office of Bank Charters and Compliance

12. As of December 2000, what percent of all U.S. banks had state charters?
    a. 92%
    b. 73%
    c. 50%
    d. 6%

13. Approximately what percent of U.S. banks choose to be covered by the FDIC?
    a. 97.5%
    b. 92.0%
    c. 73.1%
    d. 5.4%

14. Which of the following decades saw the greatest number of bank failures?
    a. the 1950s
    b. the 1960s
    c. the 1970s
    d. the 1980s

15. Which of the following would tend to increase competition?
    a. limiting banks to one branch, with that branch required to be within 1 mile of the home offices of the bank
    b. allowing banks to open new branches whenever and wherever the banks judge the branches can be profitable
    c. forcing all banks operating in a state to have one, and only one, branch in each county of that state
    d. none of the above

16. Which of the following are true?
    a. the smallest 58.2 percent of all banks own less than 4% of total banking assets
    b. the largest 5% of banks own approximately 83% of total banking assets
    c. the smallest 97.8% of banks own less than 22% of total banking assets
    d. all of the above are true

FILL IN QUESTIONS

1. In order to qualify as a bank holding company, at least one of subsidiaries of the holding company must be a _____.

2. Federal regulation of U.S. banks typically were responses to various economic crises in U.S. history, especially the crisis known as the _____.

3. When applying for a federal bank charter, the applicant must demonstrate knowledge of the business of _____ and have a substantial supply of _____ funds.

4. The _____ Act required national banks to obey the branching laws of the states the banks operated in.

5. If a bank holding company owns more than one bank, it is called a _____ holding company.

6. A bank holding company can declare itself to be a _____ and then be allowed to engage in securities underwriting and dealing.

7. As of December of 2000, branches of foreign banks controlled more than _____ percent of banking assets in the U.S.

8. When a potential borrower knows more about the risks and returns of a loan than does the bank that is considering extending the loan, the bank faces the problem of _____ _____.

9. _____ _____ problems arise when borrowers use the funds from a loan in a more risky manner than stated on the loan application.

10. The least creditworthy borrowers are most likely to try hardest to convince the bank to extend loans to them. This is the essence of the _____ _____ problem.

ESSAY QUESTIONS

1. Bank holding companies are regulated primarily by the Federal Reserve. Suppose a BHC owned several banks, one of which was state chartered. Further suppose that the Federal Reserve, but not the FDIC, imposed some new level or type of regulation on the BHC that it did not like. Could the BHC "spin-off" the state-chartered bank, making it a separate entity, now regulated primarily by the FDIC and/or the state bank examiner? Write down at least one benefit to the U.S. economy that could be traced to banks' ability to "shop around" for the most attractive regulator. Then write down at least one social cost.

2. In the United States, there has always been substantial fear of the concentrated power of large banks and large financial institutions. Or, at least, politicians and others have expressed such fears (for example, see Andrew Jackson and the First Bank of the U.S. or consider the motivation behind the McFadden Act). In spite of such fears, a relatively small number of very large financial institutions do dominate U.S. banking. Do such fears still operate today? For example, do you see more articles in your local newspaper expressing concern about the concentration of the banking industry or about the concentration of automobile production, or the concentration in the energy sector, or in pharmaceuticals? What, if anything, might cause the trend to fewer but bigger banks to reverse?

3. The federal government, through the FDIC, has indeed guaranteed the safety of bank deposits, within certain limits. While such guarantees allow depositors to have peace of mind, and the guarantees have virtually eliminated bank runs, do they also have a downside? In particular, will depositors care about the risks of the bank they deal with? So, if depositors will not monitor the risks the bank undertakes, who will? (Hint: who will be forced to pay if the bank fails?)

INTERNET EXERCISES

1. The Office of the Comptroller of the Currency charters national banks and is the primary regulator of national banks that are not bank holding companies. The OCC Web site is - http://www.occ.treas.gov. Go to the site and click on "Public Information." Find the "enforcement action" link within the text and click on it. Then select "Cease and Desist Orders" from the "Bank Actions" menu and click on "Search." Let's hope your bank is not on the list! Then click on the "Issuance" link in the left column. Then follow the "Alerts – 2001" link. Anything of interest?

2. The FDIC is perhaps the most successful federal agency. Its Web site is - http://www.fdic.gov/index.html. Click on "Are My Deposits Insured?" Then click on "Unclaimed Funds" to see if it's your turn to "hit the lottery." No luck? I didn't have any unclaimed funds, either. Try the "Electronic Deposit Insurance Estimator." Then look at the frequently asked questions (FAQ) on the EDIE page. Can you find ways to insure more than $100,000 of bank deposits?

16

Savings Associations and Credit Unions

SUMMARY

1. Savings associations such as savings banks and savings and loan associations (S&Ls), along with credit unions, are known as "thrifts." The historical role of thrifts was to accept deposits from relatively poor individuals and make mortgage loans to, again, mostly lower and middle income workers. Think of the "Bailey Bros. Building and Loan Association" in the classic Christmas movie "It's a Wonderful Life."

2. But don't wax too romantic. Not all of the folks running S&Ls were as noble of spirit as George Bailey was in the movie. In fact, the people running at least a few S&Ls in the 1980 were simply, well, criminals (see, among others, Charles Keating). The essence of an S&L is to borrow at low rates (i.e., at low passbook savings rates) and lend at higher rates (mortgage rates). A nice tidy way to make a living in normal times. However, when the inflation of the late 1970s and early 1980s touched off wild swings in interest rates and when the rates S&Ls had to pay to retain deposits exceeded the returns on their mortgages, disaster loomed. Many of the risk-reducing tools thrifts now have to manage interest rate risk were not well known or readily available twenty years ago. The S&Ls began to fail and fail in large numbers. Congress and the President attempted to help save the industry, but the new laws did as much bad as good. For example, the new laws allowed the S&L industry to make risky investments such as direct ownership (equity) investments. And the loosened regulations attracted some unsavory characters to the industry imposing significant moral hazard and adverse selection problems on the old FSLIC (the S&L equivalent of FDIC). By the time the dust settled, the U.S. taxpayers were out some $124 billion, FSLIC had been rolled into the FDIC, and the Office of Thrift Supervision had been created to regulate what was left of the industry.

3. Credit unions are nonprofit, member-owned depository institutions. Most are federally chartered. They are tax exempt. All members of a credit union must have a "common bond," such as the same employer, church, or geographic area. Most credit unions are small. The largest 7% of credit unions control 65% of credit union assets. Credit unions are regulated by the National Credit Union Association and their deposits are insured by the National Credit Union Share Insurance Fund. In the event of a temporary liquidity crisis, credit unions can draw on the Central Liquidity Facility (similar in concept to the Fed's discount window).

TRUE/FALSE QUESTIONS

T F   1.   There are actually more credit unions in the United States than there are commercial banks.

T F   2.   Historically, savings banks and savings and loans invested primarily in mortgages.

T F   3.   Credit unions do not pay income taxes.

T F   4.   All U.S. credit unions are chartered by the federal government.

T F   5.   More than half of all U.S. savings banks are located in New York and Massachusetts.

T F   6.   Savings banks, savings and loans, and credit unions are all eligible for coverage by the FDIC.

T F   7.   While the number of saving institutions has fallen by more than 50% from the early 1980s, the total assets of savings banks and S&Ls has remained about the same as in the 1980s.

T F   8.   During the years when Regulation Q limited the interest financial institutions could pay on deposits, S&Ls were allowed to pay up to one-half percentage point higher interest on passbook savings than commercial banks were allowed to pay.

T F   9.   The inversion of interest rates in the late 1970s, when short-term rates exceeded long-term rates, was the primary reason for the subsequent S&L crisis.

T F   10. Credit unions are not allowed to make mortgage loans.

T F   11. In response to the S&L crisis, laws passed in the early 1980s tightened S&L capital requirements and imposed new restrictions regarding the creditworthiness of borrowers seeking loans from S&Ls.

T F   12. Share draft accounts are credit union equivalents to checking accounts.

T F   13. By the end of 2000, more than 66% of American households owned their own homes.

T F   14. Mortgages are secured by land and real property.

T F   15. The number of credit unions has declined over the past thirty years.

T F   16. Federally chartered credit unions may choose to join the Federal Reserve System.

T F   17. Savings banks and S&Ls may choose to join the Federal Reserve System.

T F   18. Adjustable rate mortgages reduce the interest rate risk faced by thrifts.

T F   19. Adjustable rate mortgages increase the default risk faced by thrifts.

MULTIPLE CHOICE QUESTIONS

1. Savings associations engage in all of the following activities except:
   a. investing in mortgages
   b. making automobile loans
   c. underwriting initial public offerings
   d. investing in Treasury bills

2. Savings associations engage in all of the following activities except:
   a. accepting demand deposits (checking accounts)
   b. accepting time deposits
   c. accepting savings deposits
   d. accepting mineral deposits

3. Legislation passed in the early 1980s in response to the developing S&L crisis:
   a. imposed greater regulatory oversight on the S&Ls
   b. allowed the S&Ls to reduce the amount of capital required to meet solvency regulations
   c. restricted the entities S&Ls could lend to in an attempt to reduce their risk exposure
   d. forbade the S&Ls from raising the rates they offered on savings accounts

4. The primary financial regulator of thrifts is:
   a. the Office of Thrift Supervision
   b. the Federal Reserve
   c. the Thrift Regulation and Control Corporation
   d. the Federal Deposit Insurance Corporation

5. The Savings Association Insurance Fund is a subsidiary of:
   a. the Office of Thrift Supervision
   b. the Federal Reserve
   c. the Thrift Regulation and Control Corporation
   d. the Federal Deposit Insurance Corporation

6. Thrifts are most at risk from:
   a. rising interest rates
   b. short-term rates falling below mortgage rates
   c. falling interest rates
   d. mortgage rates falling below short-term rates

7. The credit union equivalent of a central bank is:
   a. the Credit Central Corporation
   b. the U.S. Central Credit Union
   c. the Federal Reserve Bank
   d. the Central Pacific Credit Union

Chapter 16 — Savings Associations and Credit Unions

8. Reflecting the fact that the members of the credit union mutually own the credit union, credit union deposits are called:
   a. deposits
   b. mutual funds
   c. shares
   d. certificates

9. Interest paid on credit union deposits is truly interest but it is referred to as:
   a. dividends
   b. certificate receipts
   c. shares
   d. interest

10. Credit unions invest in:
    a. mortgage loans
    b. government securities
    c. automobile and other consumer loans
    d. all of the above

11. Which of the following is nearest to the percentage of U.S. households that own their own homes?
    a. 92%
    b. 81%
    c. 77%
    d. 66%
    e. 14%

12. If credit unions lose their nonprofit status and become subject to paying income tax, holding all other factors equal:
    a. the rates they pay depositors would likely fall
    b. the rates they charge on loans would likely increase
    c. the rate of growth in credit union assets would likely slow
    d. all of the above

13. In Japan, the largest near-equivalent to U.S. thrifts, at least on the savings side, is run by:
    a. the Tokyo Stock Exchange
    b. the Japanese Post Office
    c. the Bank of Japan
    d. the Nikkei Central Credit Union

14. Mortgage loans with loan-to-value ratios exceeding 80%:
    a. can be made if insured by the Veterans Administration
    b. require private mortgage insurance (PMI), if the mortgage is a conventional mortgage
    c. are considered to be highly leveraged loans
    d. all of the above

15. The credit union equivalent of a checking account is:
    a. a share certificate account
    b. a share draft account
    c. a share demand account
    d. a share and share alike account

FILL IN QUESTIONS

1. A _____ savings bank does not issue stock, but is instead owned and controlled by its savings depositors.
2. Deposits in most S&Ls are insured by the _____ _____ _____ _____ (SAIF).
3. The credit union equivalent of a certificate of deposit (CD) is a _____.
4. A credit union facing an emergency liquidity crisis would turn to the _____ for assistance.
5. In Quebec, a _____ would be called a "caisse populaire," and would have many of the same restrictions as in the U.S., including the requirement that all members share a common bond.

ESSAY QUESTIONS and INTERNET EXERCISES

1. The S&L crisis could have been handled at a relatively low cost if the federal government would have injected money into the FSLIC in the early 1980s. Why did the politicians of the day choose to not spend the money? For answers, try these Web sites:

   a. An article in the fedgazette of the Minneapolis Fed - http://minneapolisfed.org/pubs/fedgaz/fg/edi909a.html.

   b. An article by William H. Starbuck, New York University and P. Narayan Pant, National University of Singapore - http://www.stern.nyu.edu/%7Ewstarbuc/sl/trying.html.

   c. An article by Rodger Citron - http://writ.news.findlaw.com/commentary/20010518_citron.html.

2. Credit unions are tax-exempt. Credit unions are, supposedly, small, member-owned nonprofits. However, take a look at the Pentagon Federal Credit Union Web site - http://www.penfed.org. Click on "News" and then on the "2000 Annual Report" and you'll see, on page 6 of the report, that PFCU has over $3.6 billion in assets. Refer back to the chart giving commercial bank asset sizes in Chapter 15 and you'll also see that PFCU would be about the 180th largest bank in the U.S. Click on "Join" and learn the membership requirements to join PFCU. Would you describe these membership requirements as difficult to meet? Now try the Navy Federal Credit Union - http://www.navyfcu.org. Click on "How to Join." Is it easier or more difficult to join the Navy

Federal Credit Union? Click on "About Navy Federal." Then load up the 2000 Annual Report. Is Navy Federal larger or smaller than Pentagon Federal? By the way, before you conclude that I "have it in" for the military credit unions, be advised that I am a member of Pentagon Federal Credit Union and two other credit unions as well and I will certainly do all I can to keep the credit unions tax-exempt.

3. Go to the CUNA Web site - http://www.cuna.org/data/index.html. Click on "Governmental Affairs" and then on "Grassroots Action Center." Why does the Credit Union National Association need a grassroots action center?

17

Regulation of the Banking and Financial Services Industry

SUMMARY

1. Who regulates whom?

    a. Federally chartered commercial banks are regulated by the Office of the Comptroller of the Currency, the FDIC, and the Federal Reserve.

    b. State banks are regulated by state banking commissioners, possibly by the Federal Reserve (refer to Chapter 15), also possibly by the FDIC (again see Chapter 15).

    c. The Federal Reserve sets the reserve requirements for all depository institutions (commercial banks, savings associations, S&Ls, and credit unions).

    d. Bank holding companies and financial holding companies are regulated by the Federal Reserve.

    e. Savings associations and S&Ls are regulated by the Office of Thrift Supervision (OTS) and, possibly, by the FDIC (see Chapter 16).

    f. Federally chartered credit unions are regulated by the National Credit Union Administration.

    g. State chartered credit unions are regulated by state banking commissioners.

    h. Credit unions are also regulated by the National Credit Union Share Insurance Fund.

    i. Finance companies require state government permission to operate, but otherwise are essentially unregulated.

    j. Financial futures contracts are regulated by the Commodity Futures Trading Commission (CFTC), an arm of the federal government, and self-regulated by a private group, the National Futures Association.

    k. Financial options are regulated by the Securities and Exchange Commission (SEC). However, options on futures are regulated by the CFTC. Self-regulation of the industry is provided by the Options Clearing Corporation (OCC).

    l. Mutual funds are regulated by the SEC.

m. Insurance companies are regulated by the states wherein they conduct business.

n. Defined benefit pension funds are regulated by the Pension Benefit Guaranty Corporation (a division of the Department of Labor) while defined contribution pension plans are regulated primarily by the Department of Labor and the Internal Revenue Service.

o. Securities markets (stocks and bonds) are regulated by the SEC. Initial margin requirements, however, are set by the Federal Reserve. Self-regulation is provided by the National Association of Securities Dealers (NASD) and by the exchanges. The Securities Investor Protection Corporation (SIPC), a nonprofit, independent, member-owned corporation, insures retail customer accounts.

p. Money markets are, essentially, unregulated.

2. Deregulation – Financial regulation in the U.S derives primarily from laws passed in response to the Depression of the 1930s. However, by the late 1970s, many of the 1930s era restrictions appeared to be unnecessary or ineffective. Thus, laws were passed which reduced the regulatory burden on financial institutions. Two pieces of legislation that deregulated financial markets were the Depository Institutions Deregulation and Monetary Control Act (DIDMCA) of 1980 and the Garn-St. Germain Depository Institutions Act of 1982.

    a. DIDMCA (1) phased out the Regulation Q ceilings on the rates that savings accounts could pay, (2) allowed S&Ls and savings associations to extend loans to businesses (i.e., make commercial loans), (3) allowed interest to be paid on checking accounts, (4) suspended state usury laws, (5) imposed universal reserve requirements on all depository institutions, and (6) required that the reserve requirement imposed on similar accounts at differing institutions be the same (for example, the reserve requirements on commercial bank checking accounts and those placed on credit union share drafts would be the same). Reserve requirements would thus be both universal and uniform.

    b. Garn-St. Germain allowed depository institutions to offer money market deposit accounts with limited check-writing privileges (effectively eliminating Regulation Q and allowing interest bearing checking accounts, accelerating the changes allowed under DIDMCA).

3. Re-regulation – In response to the S&L crisis of the 1980s, legislation was passed that imposed more regulation of financial institutions and markets. The Financial Institutions Reform, Recovery, and Enforcement Act (FIRREA) of 1989 and the Federal Deposit Insurance Corporation Act (FDICIA) of 1991 are two such pieces of legislation.

    a. FIRREA (1) injected $50 billion into the Savings Association Insurance Fund, the deposit insurance entity that replaced the old FSLIC. FIRREA also (2) established the Office of Thrift Supervision as the primary regulator of thrifts and created the Resolution Trust Corporation as a temporary agency to sell thrifts taken over by FSLIC and SAIF. FIRREA (3) made deposit insurance a full faith and credit obligation of the U.S. government. FIRREA (4) restricted S&L investments, forcing the S&Ls out of junk bonds and reducing their commercial lending. Finally, FIRREA (5) imposed stricter capital requirements on thrifts.

    b. FDICIA reformed the FDIC by (1) scaling insurance premiums to risk; banks with greater exposure to failure would pay higher insurance premiums. This partially solves the moral hazard problem presented by deposit insurance in which financial institutions may be tempted to engage in risky, high return activities, knowing that if they fail, Uncle Sam will bail them out. FDICIA also (2) set basic deposit insurance coverage at $100,000 per regular account. It (3) required the FDIC to generally use the least costly (to the government) method of resolving a bank insolvency, even if it means permanently closing the bank or S&L. It (4) categorized banks by strength of capitalization and directed greater supervision to undercapitalized banks. Finally, FDICIA (5) restricted deposit insurance on some foreign bank deposits.

4. Basel Accord – In 1988, the major trading nations agreed to international standards for bank capitalization. The idea was to reduce the risk of bank failure and to standardize certain bank regulation across national borders (facilitating trade, lending, etc.). The agreement established standards for "core capital" and for "total capital." Core capital is, by definition, the historical value of outstanding stock plus retained earnings. Total capital is core capital plus loan-loss reserves plus subordinated debt. Under the accord, capital must be a certain percent of bank assets. But not all bank assets are always treated equally. Capital is first measured against risk-adjusted assets. Low-risk assets (government securities, reserves) are not required to have any capital held against the low risk asset. Medium-risk assets are partially exempt from the capital requirements (mortgages are treated as if they are 50% of face value and interbank deposits are only 20% of face value). High-risk assets (loans and letters of credit) are 100% of face value. Core capital must be at least 4% of the risk-adjusted assets and total capital must be at least 8% of risk-adjusted capital. As an additional test, core capital must be at least 3% of total assets measured without any risk adjustment.

5. Other legislation affecting financial institutions – The Community Reinvestment Act of 1977 was designed to improve the availability of credit in economically disadvantaged areas. The Interstate Banking and Branching Efficiency Act of 1994 eliminated restrictions on interstate bank branching. The Gramm-Leach-Bliley Act (GLBA) of 1999 effectively repealed the Glass-Steagall Act. Under GLBA, bank holding companies (BHCs) meeting certain conditions can declare themselves to financial holding companies (FHCs). FHCs may engage in underwriting, insurance agency, and merchant banking, as well as commercial banking.

TRUE/FALSE QUESTIONS

T F 1. The Gramm-Leach-Bliley Act (GLBA) eliminated Federal Reserve regulation of bank holding companies (BHCs).

T F 2. The primary regulator of state chartered credit unions is the Office of Thrift Supervision (OTS).

T F 3. The primary regulator of federally chartered credit unions is the Office of Thrift Supervision (OTS).

T F 4. Reserve requirements for both national and state chartered credit unions are set by the NCUA.

T F 5. The primary regulators of nationally chartered commercial banks are the Comptroller of the Currency, the FDIC, and the Federal Reserve System.

Chapter 17   Regulation of the Banking and Financial Services Industry

T F   6.   Reserve requirements for S&Ls are set by the Office of Thrift Supervision.

T F   7.   A bank with $8,000,000 of core capital has the following assets: loans of $100,000,000, mortgages of $75,000,000, reserves of $25,000,000, and government securities of $75,000,000. This bank fails to meet the core capital as a percent of risk-adjusted assets test.

T F   8.   A bank with $8,000,000 of core capital has the following assets: loans of $100,000,000, mortgages of $75,000,000, reserves of $25,000,000, and government securities of $75,000,000. This bank fails to meet the core capital as a percent of total (i.e., not risk-adjusted) assets test.

T F   9.   FIRREA dissolved the FSLIC.

T F   10. FDICIA dissolved the FDIC.

T F   11. Under FIRREA, most Federal Reserve regulatory functions were placed under the aegis of the Office of Thrift Supervision.

T F   12. One example of moral hazard is a bank's increased willingness to make risky loans knowing that if the loans fail the FDIC will pay off the bank's depositors.

T F   13. Redlining refers to the increased regulatory supervision given to unprofitable banks, banks that are said to be operating "in the red."

T F   14. Under the Community Reinvestment Act, FHCs are obligated to increase the availability of credit in economically disadvantaged areas.

T F   15. Most credit union deposits are insured by the FDIC.

T F   16. The Pension Benefit Guaranty Corporation (Penny Benny) regulates defined contribution pension plans.

T F   17. Under the Basel Accord, money markets are primarily regulated by the Bank for International Settlements.

T F   18. Two examples of deregulation are FIRREA and DIDMCA.

T F   19. Under FIRREA, S&Ls were required to sell off their junk bond investments.

T F   20. Under FDICIA, the FDIC was required to always use "the purchase and assumption method" in dealing with failed financial institutions.

MULTIPLE CHOICE QUESTIONS

1. Which of the following made deposit insurance a full faith and credit obligation of the federal government?
   a. FIRREA
   b. GLBA
   c. FDICIA
   d. Garn-St. Germain

2. All of the following might regulate state chartered banks except:
   a. the Federal Reserve
   b. the FDIC
   c. state bank examiners
   d. the OTS

3. Which of the following pieces of legislation would be characterized as "re-regulation?"
   a. FDICIA
   b. GLBA
   c. Garn-St. Germain
   d. IBBEA

4. Which of the following pieces of legislation suspended state usury ceilings?
   a. FIRREA
   b. FDICIA
   c. Garn-St. Germain
   d. DIDMCA
   e. none of the above

5. Which of the following pieces of legislation imposed universal and uniform reserve requirements on depository institutions?
   a. FIRREA
   b. FDICIA
   c. Garn-St. Germain
   d. DIDMCA
   e. none of the above

6. Which of the following imposed uniform international capital standards on the global banking system?
   a. GLBA
   b. the Basel Accord
   c. the Bretton Woods Agreement
   d. the International Bank Capital Standards Agreement

7. Consider a bank with the following assets: $100 million of commercial loans, $250 million of mortgages, reserves of $18 million, government securities of $15 million, and standby letters of credit of $85 million. Under the Basel Accord, the bank would need how many dollars of core capital to meet the "risk-adjusted" assets test.
   a. $22.1 million
   b. $19.4 million
   c. $15.6 million
   d. $12.4 million

8. Consider a bank with the following assets: $100 million of commercial loans, $250 million of mortgages, reserves of $18 million, government securities of $15 million, and standby letters of credit of $85 million. Under the Basel Accord, the bank would need how many dollars of core capital to meet the not risk –adjusted total assets test.
   a. $22.1 million
   b. $19.4 million
   c. $14,1 million
   d. $11.5 million

9. Consider a bank with the following assets: $100 million of commercial loans, $250 million of mortgages, reserves of $18 million, government securities of $15 million, and standby letters of credit of $85 million. Under the Basel Accord, the bank would need how many dollars of total capital to meet the "risk-adjusted" assets test.
   a. $24.8 million
   b. $19.4 million
   c. $14.1 million
   d. $12.4 million

10. Which of the following is most closely associated with the "too big to fail" doctrine?
    a. purchase and assumption method
    b. the New York Yankees payroll
    c. the payoff method
    d. the Basel Accord

11. Which of the following pieces of legislation effectively repealed the Glass-Steagall Act?
    a. GLBA
    b. FIRREA
    c. FDICIA
    d. DIDMCA

12. Which of the following replaced the Federal Home Loan Bank Board?
    a. RTC
    b. OTS
    c. FDIC
    d. NCUA

Chapter 17 Regulation of the Banking and Financial Services Industry

13. Which of the following imposed risk-adjusted deposit insurance premiums on depository institutions?
    a. DIDMCA
    b. FIRREA
    c. FDICIA
    d. the Basel Accord

14. Which of the following pieces of legislation had as one of its objectives elimination of redlining?
    a. DIDMCA
    b. FIRREA
    c. CRA
    d. the Basel Accord

15. Financial holding companies (FHCs) were authorized under:
    a. DIDMCA
    b. GLBA
    c. CRA
    d. the Basel Accord

FILL IN QUESTIONS

1. Most financial deregulation occurred _____ the S&L crisis of the middle 1980s.

2. Passed in 1980, _____ increased deposit insurance from $40,000 to $100,000 per account.

3. The _____ regulates international bank capital standards.

4. Securities exchanges are primarily regulated by the _____.

5. The _____ sets initial margin requirements for securities trading.

6. S&Ls are primarily regulated by the _____.

7. Mutual funds are primarily regulated by the _____.

8. Re-regulation of the financial markets was, at least in part, a response to the _____ of the middle 1980s, a crisis that eventually bankrupted the FSLIC.

9. Under the Basel Accord, only _____ percent of interbank deposits are counted as assets under the risk-adjusted assets approach.

10. A bank holding company can declare itself to be a _____ and then be allowed to engage in securities underwriting and dealing.

ESSAY QUESTIONS

1. The risk-adjustment of the Basel Accord treats government securities as having zero risk. Is this a fair and correct approach? Are such securities truly risk-free? Also, is there a conflict of interest in having governments tell banks that government securities do not require capital to be held against the securities? Does such treatment make it easier for governments to sell government securities to the banks?

2. Explain why it is true that the "too big to fail" practice sometimes used by the FDIC prior to the passage of the FDICIA effectively insured all deposits, not just deposits up to $100,000 per account.

3. If banks practice racial discrimination by making it more difficult for blacks or other minorities to get loans, what should be true about the default rates on loans made to black applicants versus default rates on loans made to whites? That is, if less than well-qualified blacks are denied loans, but less than well-qualified whites are given loans, which group should evidence higher default rates?

INTERNET EXERCISES

1. A somewhat colorful description of the moral hazard problem of deposit insurance can be found at http://www.aci.net/kalliste/zombie.htm. What solutions to this problem exist?

2. The Securities Industry Association represents the interests of its member investment banks and stock exchanges in hearings before Congress and operates as a self-regulator. Its Web site is http://www.sia.com. Click on "Key Issues" and then "Gramm-Leach-Bliley" to get the SIA perspective on the impact of GLBA.

18

Insurance Companies

SUMMARY

1. Risk exists when that which can happen can differ from that which is expected to happen. More precisely, risk exists when we can reasonably assess the probabilities associated with the various outcomes that are possible. Uncertainty, on the other hand, exists when we cannot specify the probabilities associated with possible outcomes. Insurance companies have made themselves experts at assessing and managing various risks. The most important principle underlying insurance is the principle of "pooling of risk." Suppose that an insurance company can reasonably expect that 4 houses out of 1,000 houses will burn down over the next year. Suppose, for simplicity, that we live in a community with 1,000 houses and that each house is worth $100,000. Thus, $400,000 of loss to fire is expected over the next year. If the insurance company writes fire coverage for all 1,000 houses and charges each homeowner a $400 premium, there would be enough money in the insurance pool to meet the expected loss. By pooling the risk of loss to fire, each homeowner has insured against a $100,000 loss by making only a $400 payment. Of course, if more than 4 houses burn in a given year, the pool will not be sufficient (and if fewer burn, the pool will be more than sufficient). Assessing the probability of loss and establishing the proper premium to charge to insure against such losses is the heart and soul of the insurance business.

2. The four types of professionals that work in the insurance industry are: actuaries, agents, underwriters, and claims adjusters. Actuaries use statistical analysis to assess the probability of an event occurring. Agents sell insurance policies to the customer. Underwriters review the applications sent to them by agents and approve or reject the policies. Claims adjusters verify losses and determine the insurance company's obligations under the policy.

3. Life insurance companies insure individuals against the risk of premature death. They don't insure people against death – sadly, everyone will die. But early death can impose substantial hardship on one's family. Some life insurance provides tax-advantaged approaches to saving. Life insurance companies also sell annuities, which help individuals manage their retirement income. The two basic types of life insurance are term and permanent (whole life). In exchange for the payment of the premium, term insurance agrees to pay the policy face value should the insured die within the term of the policy. The premium is based on the chance of dieing within the term and, of course, rises as the insured ages. Term life insurance is inexpensive when the insured is young and is especially attractive when sold as part of a group life insurance plan. Permanent life insurance stays in effect throughout the life of the insured, so long as the premiums are paid. Whole life premiums are higher than term premiums, but do not rise as the insured ages. Furthermore, whole life policies build "cash value," meaning that a portion of the premium is invested on behalf of the insured. These investments grow tax deferred, at a rate specified in the whole life contract, allowing whole life to be, partially, a tax-advantaged savings account. Variations of whole life exist that pay

135

higher returns on these savings (although the higher returns also entail, of course, higher risk). Universal life contracts invest the savings portion of the premium into money market instruments that pay a variable return, while variable life policies invest the savings into common stocks. Life insurance companies also sell annuities. An annuity is a series of payments that the insurance company promises to make to the annuitant either for the life of the annuitant or for some specified period of time. If the payments begin immediately, the annuity is called an immediate annuity. If the payments begin at a later date, the annuity is called a deferred annuity. A life annuity solves the problem of outliving your money, assuming the insurance company doesn't go into bankruptcy before you die. Life insurance companies also sell disability insurance. If the insured becomes disabled while the policy is in effect, the insurance company makes a monthly payment to the insured (replacing a portion of the insured's lost income). Finally, life insurance companies sell long-term care insurance that cover at least a portion of the costs of staying in a long-term care facility.

4. Health coverage contracts in the United States are typically referred to as health insurance policies, but they are not insurance in the proper sense of the word. Insurance covers the risk of catastrophic loss from rare events. Most Americans use health "insurance" as their primary means of everyday medical coverage. For many Americans, health coverage is provided as part of their employment compensation package. Many other Americans are without health insurance (as to whether this means they are without health *care* is a contentious issue). Health care costs have risen sharply in the past two decades (at least in part due to the perception that "someone else" (the government, the insurance company) pays when one seeks medical care.

5. Property and casualty insurers protect insured property from loss and provide protection for liabilities arising from accidents. Homeowners insurance and automobile insurance are the two most important types of P&C insurance.

6. Insurance companies are regulated by the states wherein they do business. There is, essentially, no federal regulation of the insurance industry. The two biggest problems facing insurance companies are adverse selection and moral hazard. Adverse selection occurs when those seeking insurance coverage are more likely to file a claim than is the general population. For example, an individual with a terminal illness and only a month to live might try to buy a $10,000,000 term life insurance policy. Moral hazard occurs when those insured take less care to safeguard their property because it is insured. For example, one leaves the car key in the ignition thinking that if it's stolen, it's insured. To guard against adverse selection and moral hazard, insurance companies screen applicants and refuse to underwrite policies on those in poor health or who have bad driving records. Another approach would be to charge higher premiums to smokers, say, or bad drivers, to compensate the insurance company for the increased likelihood of a claim being filed. Insurers also require deductibles, so that the insured shares at least part of the loss (and thus takes greater care to avoid such losses). Coinsurance also forces the insured to pay part of the loss and is often used to discourage policyholders from seeking needless medical care. Companies can cancel coverage if the policyholder files too many claims. Companies exclude certain losses from coverage (losses from war, for example) and deny coverage to injuries sustained while engages in risky behavior (such as skydiving). Insurance companies hire investigators to investigate potential fraudulent claims and limit insurance to the actual loss suffered (you can't file a $200,000 claim on a $100,000 loss due to a house fire, even if you insured the house for $200,000). Reinsurance companies, in effect, insure insurance companies, thus carrying the concept of pooling exposures to a higher level.

Chapter 18 — Insurance Companies

TRUE/FALSE QUESTIONS

T F 1. Because most people are risk averse, they prefer the certain loss of paying a small insurance premium to the unlikely but very costly loss which is covered by the insurance policy.

T F 2. An example of the problem of moral hazard is a homeowner who fails to trim overhanging tree branches from hitting the roof of his house, as any damage from the branches is covered by his homeowner's policy.

T F 3. The fundamental principle that underlies insurance is the principle of risk identification.

T F 4. Insurance companies earn revenue both from the premiums they charge and from the financial assets purchased using premium dollars not paid as claims.

T F 5. While insurance companies are allowed to recognize premiums as revenue, they are required to rebate to policyholders any income earned from investing the premiums.

T F 6. Deliberately setting fire to an insured building is an example of adverse selection.

T F 7. An independent insurance agent sells only the products of one particular insurance company.

T F 8. Between 1989 and 1998, the proportion of U.S. families that own at least one life insurance policy has declined.

T F 9. Whole life insurance requires that a single premium covering the entire period of the policy (the "whole" period) be paid at the initiation of the policy.

T F 10. Term life insurance expires worthless at the end of the term of coverage.

T F 11. A variable life insurance policy allows the insured to earn money market rates of return on the savings portion of the premiums paid.

T F 12. A universal life insurance policy allows the insured to earn money market rates of return on the savings portion of the premiums paid.

T F 13. Life insurance policies wherein the savings portion of the premium is invested into common stocks are known as annuity policies.

T F 14. Health Maintenance Organizations provide almost complete health care coverage at a fixed per person premium, subject to deductible and copayment provisions.

T F 15. Although there are more property and casualty insurers than there are life insurance companies, the total assets of the life insurance industry exceed those of the P&C industry.

T F 16. The insurance industry is unregulated.

Chapter 18   Insurance Companies

T F   17. Most policyholders would not file a claim on a property loss that was less than the amount of the deductible per claim.

T F   18. Coinsurance reduces moral hazard by requiring the policyholder to share a portion of the burden of a claim.

T F   19. The National Association of Insurance Commissioners has succeeded in developing models laws and regulations for the various state legislatures such that only slight variations exist from state to state regarding insurance policies and practices.

T F   20. In order to legally sell insurance products in a state, the insurance agent wishing to sell the products must be licensed by that state.

MULTIPLE CHOICE QUESTIONS

1. Male drivers under the age of 21 are often charged higher premiums for automobile insurance than female drivers under the age of 21. This is an example of insurance companies:
   a. bias
   b. use of actuaries to analyze statistical evidence of risk (young males tend to have more accidents than young females)
   c. use of independent agents
   d. response to regulatory pressure to keep male drivers off public roads

2. Establishing the probability that a 47-year-old female who does not smoke will die within the next year is a function of:
   a. morticians
   b. claims adjusters
   c. morbid people
   d. actuaries

3. Financial liabilities arising from your dog having bitten the neighbor's child would be covered by:
   a. casualty insurance
   b. life insurance
   c. moral hazard
   d. Medicaid

4. Annuities are primarily sold by:
   a. life insurance companies
   b. health insurance companies
   c. property and casualty insurance companies
   d. the Social Security Administration

Chapter 18　　　　　　　　　　　　　　　　　　　　　　　　　　　　　Insurance Companies

5. Which of the following sells insurance products offered by more than one insurance company?
   a. theatrical agent
   b. independent agent
   c. exclusive agent
   d. intelligence agent

6. Which of the following life insurance contracts never builds cash value?
   a. whole life
   b. universal life
   c. variable life
   d. term life

7. Life insurance is tax advantaged in that:
   a. whole life cash values grow on a tax deferred basis
   b. life insurance premiums are always tax deductible
   c. death benefits on life insurance policies usually pass to the named beneficiary without being subject to income tax
   d. a and c
   e. all of the above

8. Which of the following life insurance types shift the risk that the invested assets fail to earn the expected return from the insurance company onto the policyholder?
   a. universal life
   b. variable life
   c. whole life
   d. a and b
   e. all of the above

9. In addition to life insurance policies, life insurance companies also sell:
   a. disability insurance
   b. annuities
   c. long-term care insurance
   d. a and c
   e. all of the above

10. A typical health coverage policy would pay all or part of:
    a. hospitalization
    b. visits to a doctor's office
    c. laboratory tests
    d. all of the above
    e. none of the above

11. Most automobile insurance combines:
    a. life and casualty insurance
    b. property and life insurance
    c. casualty and property insurance
    d. liability insurance and an annuity

12. Under "no-fault" automobile insurance, in the event of an accident:
    a. policyholders always collect from their own insurer
    b. policyholders only collect from their insurer if they can prove that they were not at fault for the accident
    c. insurance companies avoid all claims for liability arising from the accident
    d. no party to the accident can ever be held liable for causing the accident
    e. a and d

13. Life insurance companies hold a greater proportion of their invested assets in the form of long-term bonds and common stocks in comparison to property and casualty insurance companies because:
    a. property and casualty companies require greater liquidity as their risk exposures are more variable than the risk exposures of life insurance companies
    b. property and casualty companies require greater liquidity due to the greater exposure P&C companies have to adverse selection and moral hazard
    c. life insurance companies benefit from the protection offered by the federal government's Life Insurance Protection Corporation (LIPC) but P&C companies do not
    d. a and b
    e. none of the above

14. One exception to the general rule that the U.S. federal government imposes little regulatory burden on the insurance industry is:
    a. the federal requirement that all employees with at least one year experience at the same firm be offered group term life insurance
    b. the federal requirement that employees not be denied health care coverage due to preexisting conditions
    c. the federal requirement that long-term care insurance only be offered to those already covered by either Medicare or Medicaid
    d. none of the above are exceptions to the general rule that the U.S. federal government imposes little regulatory burden on the insurance industry

15. Interest rate risk is of particular concern to life insurance companies because:
    a. the premiums received by the insurers are not sufficient to pay claims presented
    b. their financial assets tend to be long-term
    c. state insurance commissions generally require the companies to remain highly liquid
    d. they are almost as highly leveraged as are commercial banks

16. Many state insurance laws and regulations are patterned after those of:
    a. Ohio
    b. New York
    c. California
    d. Florida

FILL IN QUESTIONS

1. Perhaps the most recognized name in insurance, _____ started as a coffeehouse located in the merchant and shipping district of London, England.

2. _____ occurs when those most likely to file a claim are those that work hardest to acquire insurance coverage.

3. Paying an arsonist to burn an insured building is, of course, illegal. It also is an example of a _____ _____ problem.

4. Actuaries develop statistical tables that measure the likelihood that a person will die within a particular time, say one year. These tables are called _____ tables.

5. Holding all other factors constant, the premiums on _____ life insurance will be less than the premiums on _____ life insurance.

6. The savings portion of variable life insurance premiums are invested into _____ mutual funds.

7. The savings portion of universal life insurance premiums are invested into _____ mutual funds.

8. The risk of outliving your money can be eliminated through the purchase of a _____.

9. As more and more financial holding companies enter into both commercial banking and insurance, journalists have a coined a new term to describe the combined businesses: _____.

10. Most people are _____ when it comes to risk, which explains why they are willing to buy insurance to reduce those risks.

ESSAY QUESTIONS

1. Describe the problems that might arise if an insurance company were to offer disability insurance that offered to pay a monthly disability payment equal to or greater than the policyholder's actual salary from working.

2. Think of a risk that would be difficult to pool. What characteristic would such a risk possess? Why do insurers exclude claims based on war, floods, hurricanes, etc. from coverage?

INTERNET EXERCISES

1. Go to the Insurance Information Institute Web site - http://www.iii.org. Click on "Hot Topics." Well, what does pass for hot topics in the insurance 'biz?

2. The National Association of Insurance Commissioners Web site - http://www.naic.org - contains information for consumers, regulators and insurance companies. Click on "General" and then "Employment Opportunities" to see if the perfect job for you has just been advertised. Go back to the "General" menu and click on "Gramm-Leach-Bliley" to get the NAIC take on this most important piece of legislation.

19

Pension Plans and Finance Companies

SUMMARY

1. Pension Plans

   a. Defined benefit pension plans promise to pay workers a stated benefit upon retirement. The benefits often vary depending on age at retirement and years of service with the firm. Defined contribution pension plans, on the other hand, place a stated amount per period into the retirement fund, which is then invested in financial assets. Under defined benefit plans, the risk that investment results will not support the promised benefit remains with the employer. Under defined contribution, the employer makes no promise as to the future value of the retirement fund and all investment risk shifts to the employee. Defined contribution plans have grown dramatically over the past two decades, but fewer and fewer companies offer defined benefit plans.

   b. Pension plans may be sponsored by private entities (corporations, unions, etc.) or by government at the federal, state, and local levels. Pension funds have grown rapidly over the past decades and are now the largest equity investor among the types of financial institutions.

      1) Individual retirement accounts (IRAs) provide many Americans with a tax advantaged method of saving for their retirement. For many low and middle income earners, deposits to a traditional IRA account are tax deductible. Even if the deposits are not tax deductible, the savings grow tax deferred until withdrawn. Roth IRAs reverse the tax sequence of traditional IRAs. In a Roth IRA, deposits are made with after-tax dollars, but are tax free when withdrawn during retirement.

      2) Keogh plans provide self-employed individuals with tax advantaged retirement accounts, while SIMPLE plans are designed to help small businesses offer retirement benefits to their employees.

      3) 401(k) plans are a type of defined contribution plan that have grown rapidly in recent years. 401(k)s are portable; an employee can carry them from one employer to another. 401(k)s are tax advantaged; contributions to 401(k)s are tax deductible and grow tax deferred. Often, employers match employee contributions, providing strong incentive to participate in the plans.

   c. The Employee Retirement Income Security Act (ERISA) was signed into law in 1974. The act created the Pension Benefit Guarantee Corporation (PBGC) to regulate defined benefit pension plans. The act required employers offering defined benefit plans to make minimum contributions

Chapter 19   Pension Plans and Finance Companies

to the pension fund such that the fund was actuarially sound (i.e., able to meet its projected pension obligations). The PBGC also insures these pension plans in a manner similar to FDIC deposit insurance. Although defined contribution plans also must comply with ERISA provisions, the regulatory burden placed on defined contribution plans is light compared to the burden placed on defined benefit plans. This, in part, explains why defined contribution plans have grown more rapidly than have defined benefit plans.

2. Social Security is a U.S. federal government program that provides retirement benefits, benefits for survivors and dependents, disability benefits, and Medicare benefits to eligible individuals. Social Security is funded through a payroll tax levied on most U.S. employees and employers. The tax is 12.4% of income below $80,401 (to fund old age, survivors, and disability payments) and a further tax of 2.9% of all income (this tax funds Medicare). Over the next twenty years or so, the number of workers per Social Security recipient will fall from approximately 3 to 1 to only 2 to 1 (there were more than 30 workers per recipient in 1940). Thus, each worker will need to bear a greater proportionate burden of retires and other Social Security beneficiaries. Various proposals have been offered to reform Social Security in light of these unquestioned demographic facts. Most obvious, perhaps, is to simply raise taxes. However, payroll taxes make it more expensive to hire workers and, conceivably, might increase unemployment. Not exactly the desired result. Other proposals include raising the retirement age (again), means testing benefits (i.e., not allowing "wealthy" workers to collect full benefits), and privatizing the system (as was done in Chile in the 1980s). Of course, the least painful solution is to have the economy grow so rapidly that workers become so productive that providing benefits to a large number of retirees does not impinge greatly on the workers' well being. But which economic policies are likeliest to lead to this high, sustained growth? Well, that's a whole 'nother set of arguments.

3. Finance companies make consumer loans (cars, household durables), loans to businesses to finance inventory and accounts receivable, arrange leases of aircraft, automobiles, etc., and make real estate loans, especially sub-prime real estate loans. Finance companies acquire funds by issuing bonds, commercial paper, and borrowing from commercial banks. Finance companies tend to serve higher risk borrowers and their loans tend to have higher interest rates.

TRUE/FALSE QUESTIONS

T F   1. All Americans, whether employed or unemployed, are covered by the old age (i.e. retirement) provisions of Social Security.

T F   2. Public employee pension funds account for more than one-half of the total assets of U.S. pension funds.

T F   3. Pension funds have relatively low demand for liquidity. Consequently, most pension funds hold primarily long-term financial assets such as common stocks and long-term corporate debt.

T F   4. Defined contribution pension plans are insured by the PBGC.

T F   5. The fastest growing pension funds in the U.S. are of the defined benefit type.

Chapter 19   Pension Plans and Finance Companies

T F   6.   Keogh plans allow small businesses to offer pension plans to their employees.

T F   7.   Contributions to Roth IRAs are not tax deductible when made; however, all withdrawals from Roth IRAs will be taxed as long-term capital gains, provided the withdrawals are made after the owner of the IRA reaches age 59+½.

T F   8.   Most defined benefit private pension plans are overfunded.

T F   9.   From the point of view of the employee, defined benefit plans have more investment risk than do defined contribution plans.

T F   10.   While 401(k) plans offer tax advantages to both the employer and the employee, so few financial assets are eligible for inclusion in a 401(k) that the plans have not proved to be very popular.

T F   11.   The category "finance companies" includes captive automotive financing entities such as General Motors Acceptance Corporation and Ford Motor Credit.

T F   12.   When a business "factors" its receivables, the business actually sells the receivables to a finance company and the finance company generally assumes the risk that the receivable will prove to be not collectible.

T F   13.   Borrowers with a poor credit history are more likely to be approved for a car loan or a similar consumer loan by a finance company than they are likely to get such a loan from a commercial bank.

T F   14.   Sub-prime real estate lending is riskier, to the lender, than are conventional mortgage loans.

T F   15.   Lending 125% of the value of a property ties the borrower to that property making it less likely that the borrower will default.

T F   16.   In non-contributory pension plans, the employer makes no contributions to the plan.

T F   17.   Social Security is funded by contributions, not taxes.

T F   18.   By the year 2035, forecasts suggest that there will be two retirees for each worker paying into Social Security.

T F   19.   Finance companies face little federal regulation, but are subject to regulation by the states they do business in.

T F   20.   On your paycheck stub, the box marked FICA tells you the amount of taxes you paid to Social Security for that pay period. While not shown on your pay stub, an equal amount will have been paid by your employer.

MULTIPLE CHOICE QUESTIONS

1. Most pension plans are:
   a. overfunded
   b. contributory
   c. non-contributory
   d. uninhibited

2. Which of the following statements is/are correct?
   a. public pension fund total assets exceed the total assets of private pension funds
   b. the largest single pension fund in the U.S. is the California Public Employees Retirement System (CALPERS)
   c. private pension funds total assets exceed the total assets of public pension funds
   d. a and c
   e. b and c

3. Withdrawals from a Roth IRA (after the owner has reached age 59+½) are, in general:
   a. taxed as capital gains
   b. not taxed
   c. taxed as ordinary income
   d. subject only to FICA taxes

4. Withdrawals from a traditional IRA (after the owner has reached age 59+½) are, in general:
   a. taxed as capital gains
   b. not taxed
   c. taxed as ordinary income
   d. subject only to FICA taxes

5. For defined contribution pension plans, the risk of underperformance of the invested assets lies with:
   a. the PBGA
   b. the employer
   c. the employee
   d. the pension fund manager

6. The primary legislation under which pension plans are regulated is:
   a. Employee Retirement Income Security Act (ERISA)
   b. FDIC Improvement Act (FIDCIA)
   c. Pension Plan Regulations Act (PPRA)
   d. Codicils for the Regulation of American Pensions (CRAP)

7. The primary federal regulator of defined benefit pension plans is:
   a. the Department of Commerce
   b. the Pension Benefit Guarantee Corporation
   c. the Department of Veterans Affairs
   d. the FDIC

8. The old age, survivors, and disability income (OASDI) portion of Social Security is:
   a. free
   b. funded solely by a progressive income tax on annual income exceeding $80,400 (as of 2001)
   c. funded solely by sales taxes
   d. funded solely by a flat tax on annual income below $80,400 (as of 2001)
   e. none of the above

9. The Medicare and Medicaid portion of Social Security is:
   a. free
   b. funded solely by a progressive income tax on annual income exceeding $80,400 (as of 2001)
   c. funded solely by sales taxes
   d. funded solely by a flat tax on annual income below $80,400 (as of 2001)
   e. none of the above

10. Social Security is a:
    a. pension plan
    b. disability insurance plan
    c. medical care plan
    d. all of the above

11. Most U.S. workers fully qualify for Social Security after:
    a. 10 years of part-time employment
    b. 10 years of full-time employment
    c. 15 quarters of employment
    d. 3 months of full time employment or 6 months of part-time employment

12. If current forecasts prove true, in 2030 there will be _____ workers for each Social Security recipient.
    a. 2
    b. 13
    c. 3
    d. ½

13. Including both OASDI tax and the Medicare tax, self-employed individuals in the U.S. pay a FICA payroll tax rate of:
    a. 38.30%
    b. 15.30%
    c. 7.65%
    d. 0.14%

14. Including both OASDI tax and the Medicare tax, most employees in the U.S. pay a FICA payroll tax rate of:
    a. 38.30%
    b. 15.30%
    c. 7.65%
    d. 0.14%

15. Many nations have public pension/insurance plans similar to Social Security, and they have many of the same problems that Social Security has. Privatization has been proposed as a potential solution to these problems. The most successful such privatization has taken place in:
    a. Thailand
    b. France
    c. Chile
    d. Morocco

16. Finance companies engage in all of the following businesses except:
    a. sub-prime real estate loans
    b. manufactured housing loans
    c. 125% equity loans
    d. underwriting municipal bonds

17. Automobile dealers often finance their inventories of new vehicles through finance companies using:
    a. lease financing
    b. mortgage loans
    c. floor plans
    d. sub-prime loans

18. Lease payments on a vehicle are often less than payments on an equivalent loan. In part, this reflects the fact that:
    a. leases provide depreciation tax benefits to the lessor that borrowers might not be able to take full advantage of
    b. leases are typically based on only a portion of the cost of the vehicle
    c. repossession of leased vehicles is easier as the lessor retains title to the vehicle
    d. all of the above

19. Finance companies that specialize in the purchase of accounts receivable of other firms are called:
    a. pawnbrokers
    b. factors
    c. brigands
    d. addends

20. PBGC insures:
    a. all pension plans
    b. defined benefit pension plans only
    c. defined contribution pension plans only
    d. sub-prime pension plans

FILL IN QUESTIONS

1. Pension plans wherein both the employee and the employer make contributions are _____ pension plans.

2. In a _____ pension, the employer makes no promises as to the specific benefit to be paid.

3. Pension plans that allow self-employed individuals to contribute a portion of their business profits to a tax deferred retirement fund are _____ plans.

4. Even if one's employer does not sponsor a pension plan, middle income Americans can still make retirement contributions with an *immediate* tax advantage by funding a _____ IRA.

5. Between 1979 and 1999, total assets in the top 100 pension plans increased from $270 billion to _____.

6. _____ make up approximately 57% of pension funds investments.

7. Traditional IRAs require withdrawals to commence at age _____.

8. Employers would be legally allowed to remove money from a defined benefit pension plan that was _____.

9. The largest manager of multi-firm defined contribution pension assets is _____.

10. Under current Social Security law and regulation, those born after 1960 must wait until age _____ before retiring with full Social Security retirement benefits.

ESSAY QUESTIONS

1. Shakespeare wrote:

    > What's in a name? That which we call a rose
    > By any other name would smell as sweet.

    But clearly the bard never met an American politician. Why is that Social Security is funded by "Federal Insurance Contribution Act" levies instead of "Federal Insurance Payroll Taxes Act" monies?

2. Let us build a rather sterile little academic world, but one that, nonetheless, has serious real world implications. I will give you two economic environments to choose from. In each, all prices of goods and services are exactly the same. In one setting, all retirees retire with exactly $3,000 per month to spend. In the other setting, ½ of 1% of retirees retire with $70,000 per month to spend and all other retirees have $3,500 per month to spend. Which scenario would you choose and why? (Hint: ask someone in your Economics Department about Pareto.)

INTERNET EXERCISES

1. First the good news – look at the Web site of the American Association of Retired People (AARP) at - http://www.aarp.org/socialsecurity. Click on the AARP "Special Report" on Social Security. What, essentially, is the AARP position on the "crisis?" But let me first ask you this question – where will the federal government get the money to redeem all those Treasury bonds in the Social Security trust funds?

2. And then the bad news – go to the Concord Coalition Web site - http://www.concordcoalition.org - and click on "Social Security Reform." Read two or three of the articles available on the page. Are you scared yet? Should you be?

   Well, which is it – impending doom or "no worries, mate?"

20

Securities Firms, Mutual Funds, and Financial Conglomerates

SUMMARY

1. Investment banks assist corporations and other issuers of financial assets in selling those assets to the public. When securities are first sold to the public, the transaction occurs in the primary market. When securities subsequently trade among the public, the transactions are said to occur in the secondary market. In an underwriting, the investment bank buys the securities from the issuer and then sells the issue to the public. The investment bank makes money as long as the price they receive from the public exceeds the price they paid to the issuer (the difference between these prices is the underwriter's spread). The very first time that an entity sells stocks or bonds (IPOs are almost always stocks, actually) to the public, the offering is an "initial public offering" or IPO. IPOs exhibit volatile behavior, often rising dramatically in the first few hours or days they trade. However, just as often, they underperform stocks with similar risks over periods beyond six months from issue. Before selling securities to the public through an investment bank, the issuer must (usually) register the securities with the SEC. The SEC does not judge the economic merits of the securities. The SEC only requires that information be disclosed, especially information regarding the use of the proceeds. This information is disclosed to the public in a document called a prospectus. To make certain that they find enough suckers, errr, investors, investment banks often organize a syndicate of several investment banks to sell the securities to the public. Subsequent to the offering, investment bankers might "make a market" in the securities. To make a market is to state to the public that you stand willing to buy or sell the securities you make a market in. Thus, market makers allow secondary market trading to occur. Note that new debt offerings far exceed new equity offerings (in part because bonds mature, while common stocks do not). Also note that if the securities are sold to one or a few institutional investors in a "private placement," most of the SEC rules regarding disclosure, etc., do not apply.

2. Secondary markets are of two types – exchanges and over-the-counter (see Chapter 11). Brokers arrange trades for their customers and earn commissions. Dealers buy and sell from their inventory and make money if, on average, they buy from the public at a lower price (the bid price) than they receive when selling to the public (the ask price). Market orders direct that the trade be executed immediately at the best prevailing price; limit orders limit the price at which one is willing to sell or to buy (but if the limit is away from the current market price, the limit order won't execute). One can borrow shares of stock from a broker, sell them, hope the price falls, then repurchase the shares at the lower price and return the shares to the broker. Such transactions are called "short sales." One

can also borrow money from a broker and use the money to purchase additional shares of stock. Such transactions are called buying stock "on margin." Stockbrokers can be "full service" brokers who will provide their customers with research and advice or "discount" brokers who will merely execute the customer's orders or they can be something in between full-service and discount.

3. While the term "mutual fund" is used to describe investment companies, in general, it really only describes open-end investment companies. Open-end investment companies sell shares directly to investors (although they often use a broker as their sales agent). Investors sell (redeem) their shares directly back to the open-end company. Purchases and redemptions are always made at net asset value (NAV), although a "load" is sometimes attached as compensation for the sales agent. The number of shares in an open-end company fluctuates from day to day depending on net purchases and redemptions. Closed-end investment companies, on the other hand, issue a fixed number of shares (in an IPO). These closed-end fund shares then trade on an exchange or OTC just as any other security would. Closed-end funds can sell for more than their NAV (at a premium) or for less than their NAV (at a discount). Both types of investment companies invest their shareholders' money into financial assets. Growth funds buy stocks, income funds buy bonds, aggressive growth funds buy smaller, riskier companies, balanced funds buy some stocks, some bonds, money market mutual funds buy money market instruments, etc.

4. Hedge funds pool the funds of their members and purchase financial assets with the money. They differ from mutual funds in that only "accredited" or "qualified" investors can invest in a hedge fund. An accredited investor has at least $1 million in investable assets, while a qualified investor has a minimum net worth of $5 million. The SEC presumes that such wealthy people are well aware of the risk involved in investing; thus, hedge funds are virtually unregulated. Hedge funds tend to be risky. They use huge amounts of debt to leverage their returns, but this leaves them exposed to bankruptcy in a market downturn. Furthermore, some hedge funds have grown so large and important that should the fund fail it would impact the entire financial system (see, for example, the trials and tribulations of Long-Term Capital Management). Thus, the issue of increased regulation of hedge funds is certain to be raised in the near future.

5. Real estate investment trusts (REITs) are closed-end investment companies that invest in either real estate or mortgages secured by real estate. REITs use debt to leverage their returns. Government sponsored enterprises (GSEs) are, or were at their onset, part of the federal government or were chartered by the U.S. Congress to achieve a social goal. For example, the Federal National Mortgage Association (Fannie Mae), the Federal Home Loan Mortgage Corporation (Freddie Mac), and the Government National Mortgage Association (Ginnie Mae) were all created by the government to issue bonds and use the proceeds to buy pools of mortgages from banks and S&Ls. The social goal was to make it easier for Americans to own homes. Freddie Mac and Fannie Mae are now private corporations and trade on the NYSE. Ginnie Mae remains part of the federal government and Ginnie Mae bonds are still backed by the full faith and credit of the U.S. Treasury. Other GSEs include the Federal Farm Credit Banks Funding Corporation and the Student Loan Marketing Association (Sallie Mae),

6. Financial conglomerates are holding companies that own several different types of financial institutions. These conglomerates often operate across national borders with subsidiaries in several countries. Economies of scale assist conglomerates. For example, the conglomerates might operate with fewer executives (only one CEO serving all the firms, for example). Conglomerates might also benefit from economies of scope in that customers can bank, buy insurance, invest in stocks, and speculate in pork bellies under one roof. Finally, conglomerates might benefit from diversification.

Chapter 20 — Securities Firms, Mutual Funds, and Financial Conglomerates

For example, a market downturn might make investment banking less profitable, but the insurance business might pick up, offsetting the loss.

TRUE/FALSE QUESTIONS

T F 1. Investment banking activities occur in the primary market. — T

T F 2. To "make a market" is to state publicly that you are willing to buy and sell from your inventory of securities that you make a market in. — T

T F 3. The first time a corporation sells its shares to the public it does so in an IPO. — T

T F 4. Prior to issuing securities to the public, issuers must register the issue with the Federal Reserve Board of Governors.   SEC — F

T F 5. The majority of open-end investment companies trade on the American Stock Exchange. — F

T F 6. Before selling securities to the public, issuing corporations must prove to the SEC that the securities offer a reasonable expected return given the risk level of the securities. — F

T F 7. If investors request to see a prospectus prior to purchasing securities issued by a corporation, the corporation must make one available to them. — F

T F 8. A group of underwriters that cooperate in bringing an issue to the public is known as an underwriting syndicate. — T

T F 9. In a typical year, more dollars of new debt are issued than dollars of new equity. — T

T F 10. Securities can only be privately placed if they are sold to qualified or accredited hedge funds. — F

T F 11. Investors that "short" the market borrow money from brokers and use the borrowed funds to buy additional securities. — F

T F 12. Open-end investment companies sometimes trade below their NAV. — F

T F 13. Balanced funds invest in some combination of Treasury bills and high-grade commercial paper. — F

T F 14. By balancing, or "hedging," their risks, hedge funds provide their investors with a financial asset which has risk characteristics similar to Treasury bills, but which pays returns nearly equal to the average return on common stocks. — F

T F 15. Sallie Mae issues bonds collateralized by pools of student loans. — T

T F 16. An "aggressive growth" mutual fund would be unlikely to own municipal revenue bonds, unless the bonds were rated below BB on the S&P rating scale. — F

Chapter 20   Securities Firms, Mutual Funds, and Financial Conglomerates

T F   17. Real estate investment trusts (REITs) are roughly equally likely to invest in commercial real estate as they are to invest in investment grade debentures.   F

T F   18. Although both Fannie Mae and Freddie Mac are wholly owned by the U.S. federal government, the common stock of both companies trades on the NYSE.   F

T F   19. Private placement of bonds occurs more often than the private placement of stocks.   T

T F   20. Dealers make money through the commissions they charge for arranging trades.   F

MULTIPLE CHOICE QUESTIONS

1. When a closed-end investment company sells for less than its NAV:
   a. pigs will fly
   b. it must re-register with the SEC
   c. it becomes an open-end investment company
   d. it is said to be trading at a discount

   D

2. Which of the following is backed by the full faith and credit of the U.S. Treasury?
   a. Ginnie Mae bonds
   b. Fannie Mae bonds
   c. Freddie Mac bonds
   d. all of the above

   A

3. The primary regulator of investment companies is the:
   a. NASD
   b. SEC
   c. NYSE
   d. Investment Company Institute

   B

4. The NAV of a closed-end investment company is 100. If the company is selling for 90 in OTC trading:
   a. it is selling at a 10% premium
   b. it is selling at a discount of 10%
   c. it is selling at a discount of 0.90
   d. it is a mistake as closed-end funds never trade below NAV

   B

5. Which of the following earn their living by charging commissions?
   a. brokers
   b. dealers
   c. principals
   d. both a and b
   e. all of the above

   A

Chapter 20 — Securities Firms, Mutual Funds, and Financial Conglomerates

6. When an open-end investment company sells for less than its NAV:
   a. pigs will fly
   b. it must re-register with the SEC
   c. it becomes an open-end investment company
   d. it is said to be trading at a discount

   A

7. All of the following are valid orders (when trading securities) except:
   a. fill quick order
   b. limit order
   c. market order
   d. all of the above are valid orders

   A

8. To purchase stocks "on margin" is to borrow money and use the proceeds of the loan to buy additional shares of stocks. The most one can initially borrow in a margin account is _____ of the value of the stocks one wishes to purchase.
   a. 100%
   b. 75%
   c. 50%
   d. 25%

   C

9. Which of the following is likely to have the lowest commissions:
   a. full service broker
   b. discount broker
   c. online broker
   d. real cheap broker

   C

10. Which of the following are characteristics of a hedge fund?
    a. high risk
    b. high expected return
    c. use of leverage (debt)
    d. all of the above

    D

11. REITs invest primarily in:
    a. commercial real estate
    b. mortgages
    c. debentures
    d. common stock
    e. a and b

    E

12. REITs are most similar to:
    a. open-end investment companies
    b. closed-end investment companies
    c. S&Ls
    d. commercial banks

    B

13. All of the following are GSEs except:
    a. the Federal Farm Credit Banks Funding Corporation
    b. Fannie Mae
    c. the Financing Corporation
    d. the Federal Farm Financing Foundation

    D

Chapter 20 Securities Firms, Mutual Funds, and Financial Conglomerates

14. A financial conglomerate would likely consist of all of the following except:
    a. a insurance company
    b. a commercial bank   C
    c. an undertaker
    d. a finance company

15. When U.S. investors buy non-U.S. securities, they tend to buy _____. When non-U.S. investors buy U.S. securities, they tend to buy _____.
    a. equities; Treasury bonds
    b. REITs; equities   A
    c. corporate bonds; equities
    d. money market instruments; Treasury bonds

FILL IN QUESTIONS

1. Securities are first issued in the _____ market and subsequently trade in the _____ market.

2. The very first time that an issuer sells securities to the public is known as an _____.

3. When a company whose stock is already actively traded among public investors sells new securities the transaction is known as a _____.

4. The document that details the company's plans for the proceeds from a new issue is the _____.

5. The _____ details the rules and restrictions that a bond issuer agrees to abide by in fulfilling the terms of a bond offering.

6. Independent, individual speculators who attempt to trade stocks for short-term gains using online trading, and who seldom carry positions for longer than a day, are known as _____.

7. The market value of an investment company's assets minus the market value of the company's liabilities, expressed on a per share basis, is the investment company's _____.

8. As of 1999, almost _____ of U.S. households owned mutual funds.

9. Financial conglomerates, because they engage in several financial markets and sell a range of financial products benefit from _____.

10. Mutual funds are primarily regulated by the _____.

ESSAY QUESTIONS and INTERNET EXERCISES

1. The mystery of why some closed-end funds trade at significant discounts has yet to be resolved. Examine the issues involved by reading the Internet Closed-End Fund Investor Web site at - http://www.icefi.com. Click on "A Guide to Investing in Closed-End Funds" (about half-way down the introductory page) and select "A Deeper Look at Discount/Premium." Find any convincing arguments that explain or justify large discounts? Then take a trip over to your local library and look up Richard Thaler's book *Behavioral Finance*. What insights do the behavioral finance theorists bring to the closed-end fund puzzle?

2. Commercial banks and savings associations often complain that the implicit government guarantee of Fannie Mae and Freddie Mac bonds gives the two GSEs an unfair advantage in competing in the mortgage loan business. Explore the issue from Fannie Mae's perspective at - http://www.fanniemae.com/news/speeches/speech_129.html. Then take a look at the American Enterprise Institute's relevant Web page for some academic discussion by going to - http://www.aei.org/nl/nlsep01.htm. Fannie Mae's competitors formed their own interest group – "FM Watch." Go to - http://www.fmwatch.org - to read their arguments alleging unfair competition from Fannie Mae and Freddie Mac. Write down the three major arguments presented by Fannie Mae in defense of GSE mortgage practices. Then write down at least three arguments of those who claim GSEs have an unfair advantage. Which, if either, side do you find more persuasive?

21

Risk Assessment and Management

SUMMARY

1. Perhaps it is obvious that one of the most important tasks for a bank is deciding to whom they will extend loans. Bankers have given a good deal of thought to credit risk (default risk) and how to manage it. Some central themes of credit risk management are:

   a. It may be acceptable to accept higher risk loans if the expected return from such loans is sufficient to compensate for the risk. That is, one seldom judges risk alone, or return alone; rather, it is the tradeoff between higher risk and higher expected returns that is crucial.

   b. Banks strive to maintain a positive spread. That is, banks want the return from their invested assets (loans, Treasury bonds, etc.) to exceed the cost of acquiring funds (deposit accounts and other liabilities).

   c. Banks use the "Five C's of Credit" to make judgments as to whether or not to grant a loan. The five C's are: capacity, character, capital, collateral, and conditions. Capacity equates to the borrower's ability to repay the loan and is typically measured by the debt-to-income ratio of the borrower. As a rough guide, the borrower's debt-to-income ratio should not exceed 36%, while, for mortgages, the housing expense-to-income ratio should not exceed 28%. Character means the willingness of the borrower to repay his or her debts. Does the borrower value his or her reputation? Capital refers to the equity stake that the borrower has in the project. The greater the capital a borrower places into a project, the less likely the borrower is to default on the loan, forfeiting most or all of that capital. Collateral is closely related to capital but here the emphasis is on what amount the lender could recognize from selling assets secured by the loan. Conditions refers to economic conditions that affect the borrower's ability to repay a loan. Even the most upstanding borrower will find it difficult to repay a loan if laid off or seriously injured.

   d. Credit scoring software allows banks and other lenders to quickly decide as to the likely creditworthiness of a borrower. These programs explain why borrowers can make a decision as to whether they will or will not extend credit within hours, sometimes within minutes, of receiving an application. The scores might also be used to price credit with those judged to be of greater default risk offered loans only at higher interest rates.

2. Most bank assets and liabilities are sensitive to changes in interest rates. Various techniques have been derived to manage this interest rate risk. One of these techniques, duration analysis, is discussed in the appendix to this chapter. Another approach is income gap analysis. Income gap analysis involves finding the difference (the gap) between the dollars of interest rate sensitive assets (ISAs) and the dollars of interest rate sensitive liabilities (ISLs). Algebraically, GAP = ISAs – ISLs. For most banks, this income gap is negative. Thus, if interest rates rise, the increased cost of funding liabilities is greater than the increased return on the assets, as the dollars of liabilities exceed the dollars of assets. Bank profits fall. The opposite is true if interest rates fall. Managing this income gap to make it unlikely that any fall in profits would endanger the solvency of the bank is an important task for bank management.

3. Liquidity risk impacts banks as the liquidity of the bank liabilities (checking deposits, savings deposits, etc.) generally exceeds the liquidity of the bank's assets (mortgages, loans, etc.). The liquidity ratio measures this risk and is calculated as: (ISAs – ISLs) / Total Assets. Typically, liquidity ratios are between plus or minus 10 percent.

4. Duration gap analysis makes use of the interest rate sensitivity measure known as duration. When interest rates go up, we know that the prices of most existing financial assets fall, but some assets are more price sensitive than others. In general, longer maturity, lower coupon assets show greater sensitivity than shorter maturity or higher coupon bonds. When interest rates go up, it should also be noted that one could reinvest any cash flows from the assets at those higher rates. This means that price risk and reinvestment risk tend to offset. If we could design a portfolio where the two risks would be equal, we could achieve a target wealth at a particular point in time regardless of whether interest rates go up or down. Duration is measured by finding, separately for each cash flow of the asset, the present value of the cash flows of the asset. Then form ratios by dividing each present value by the sum of all the present values. These ratios are then the weights associated with each period of the bond. Find the weighted average time of the bond by multiplying each period's time by their respective weight and summing. The sum is the Macaulay's duration of the asset. Algebraically:

$$\text{Duration} = \Sigma \; \frac{PV_t}{PV_{all}} * t$$

where PV_t is the present value of time t's cash flow, PV_{all} is the sum of the present values (i.e., the current price of the bond), and t equals 1, 2, 3, etc. out to the maturity of the bond. The duration of a set of assets is the weighted average of the durations of the assets where the weights are the relative values of the assets in the portfolio. Banks calculate the average duration of their assets (DURA) and the average duration of their liabilities (DURL). The duration gap is the difference between DURA and DURL: Duration gap = DURA – DURL. Most banks have a positive duration gap. When interest rates rise, a positive duration gap means that the prices of the bank's assets will fall more rapidly than the prices of the bank's liabilities. In extreme conditions, such as during the S&L crisis of the 1980s, assets will fall much faster than liabilities and the bank will become insolvent. The magnitude of the bank's exposure to interest rate risk can be measured by multiplying the duration gap by the percentage change in interest rates (the negative sign reinforces the idea that when interest rates rise, prices fall):

$$\text{percentage change in Net Worth} = - \text{duration gap} * [\Delta i / (1 + i)]$$

TRUE/FALSE QUESTIONS

T F 1. Most banks have a negative income gap.

T F 2. In normal economic environments, most banks operate with a negative interest rate spread.

T F 3. Collateral refers to the amount of equity a borrower contributes to a project.

T F 4. Capital, in a mortgage loan, is typically measured by the loan-to-value ratio.

T F 5. The larger the absolute value of the income gap, the less sensitive a bank's earning will be to changes in interest rates.

T F 6. The larger the absolute value of the duration gap, the more sensitive a bank's net worth will be to changes in interest rates.

T F 7. Default risk primarily affects the liabilities side of a bank's balance sheet.

T F 8. Capacity is typically measured by looking at the borrower's debt-to-income ratio.

T F 9. The unit of measurement for Macauley's duration is years.

T F 10. In today's rather impersonal world where borrower and lender might never meet face-to-face, a borrower's credit report forms the basic data by which banks measure the borrowers character (willingness to pay, to live up to the obligations imposed by a loan).

T F 11. In the case where a bank has a *positive* income gap, an increase in interest rates would result in an increase in the bank's profits.

T F 12. When banks divide their assets and liabilities by maturity and apply income gap analysis separately to each maturity class, the analysis is known as maturity-bucket gap analysis.

T F 13. The liquidity ratio measures the interest rate sensitivity of a bank's net worth.

T F 14. Typically, the liquidity of a bank's assets exceeds that of its liabilities.

T F 15. Duration gap analysis provides banks with a measure of their net exposure to changes in interest rates.

T F 16. A bank would have a negative duration gap if the duration of its liabilities exceeded the duration of its assets.

T F 17. When interest rates rise, cash flows can be reinvested at those higher rates. Such reinvestment can at least partially offset the price decline experienced by financial assets when interest rates rise.

T F 18. Assets with higher duration have greater price sensitivity to interest rate changes.

T F 19. If one believes that interest rates are certain to fall in the near future, one would be more likely to buy assets with shorter durations than to buy those with longer durations.

MULTIPLE CHOICE QUESTIONS

1. Calculate the duration of a bond that has three years to maturity, pays an annual coupon of 5% and has a yield to maturity of 4%.
   a. 4.5000
   b. 3.0000
   c. 2.91344
   d. 2.86146

2. A bank with a negative income gap would see its net profits increase if interest rates:
   a. rise
   b. fall
   c. remain the same
   d. become more volatile

3. A bank with a liquidity ratio of –0.25 would _____ unexpectedly large withdrawals of cash.
   a. have little or no exposure to
   b. face serious problem if exposed to
   c. actually benefit from
   d. be unable to borrow from the Fed to cover

4. All of the following are among the five C's of credit except:
   a. character
   b. competence
   c. capacity
   d. collateral

5. When banks require corporations to maintain a portion of a loan made to the corporation as a deposit in the bank, the arrangement is known as a:
   a. kickback
   b. de-leveraged loan
   c. compensating balance
   d. reserve requirement

6. Banks are more likely to make loans to less creditworthy borrowers:
   a. when the economy is growing
   b. if the banks can charge a higher interest rate to such borrowers
   c. if the loan is secured by adequate collateral
   d. all of the above

7. All of the following would be contained in a typical credit report except:
   a. current loans outstanding
   b. medical history
   c. judgments against the applicant
   d. all of the above might be found in a typical credit report

8. The use of _____ allows banks to accept or reject loans within a matter of hours.
   a. credit scores
   b. snap judgment
   c. intuition
   d. ex-ante data

9. A bank with a positive duration gap would see its net worth fall when interest rates:
   a. rise
   b. fall
   c. remain the same
   d. become more volatile

10. A bank with a duration gap of 1.2 would see its net worth _____ by _____ percent if interest rates increase from 9% to 10%.
    a. rise; 1.20000
    b. fall; 1.09091
    c. fall; 1.20000
    d. fall; 1.11092

11. A bank recalculates the duration of its liabilities and discovers that the DURL has increased. In order to maintain a duration match (i.e., to keep its duration gap equal to zero), the bank should:
    a. add more long-term loans to its portfolio
    b. reduce the number of long-term loans in its portfolio
    c. offer higher rates on its longest maturity CDs
    d. none of the above

12. If the application of credit scoring techniques has the unintentional result that fewer loans to minority applicants are approved, such credit scoring would be described as:
    a. disparate treatment
    b. overt discrimination
    c. disparate impact
    d. redlining

13. All of the following are examples of off-balance sheet items that a bank might have except:
    a. overdraft protection
    b. unused lines of credit
    c. excess reserves
    d. unused credit card balances

14. The duration of a zero coupon bond:
    a. can't be calculated
    b. is equal to its maturity
    c. always equals 1
    d. always equals 0

15. Calculate the duration of a bond that has four years to maturity, pays annual coupons of $100, has a maturity value of $1000, and is currently priced at $1,066.24254.
    a. 2.87556
    b. 3.50421
    c. 4.00000
    d. more information is needed in order to solve this question

FILL IN QUESTIONS

1. The loan-to-value ratio is most often used to measure _____ (one of the five C's of credit).

2. The debt-to-income ratio is most often used to measure _____ (one of the five C's of credit).

3. A bank's revenues are generated by its _____ side of the balance sheet.

4. As they relate to interest rate sensitivity, price and reinvestment risk are _____ related.

5. A bank with a negative duration gap is, in effect, speculating that interest rates will _____.

6. A bank becomes _____ when the value of its liabilities exceeds the value of its assets.

7. With variable rate mortgages most of the interest rate risk of the mortgage is borne by the _____.

8. Most banks have _____ income gaps.

9. Most banks have _____ duration gaps.

10. Mortgages with loan-to-value ratios of 100% to 125% are known in the trade as _____.

ESSAY QUESTIONS and INTERNET EXERCISES

1. A rather confusing and difficult to navigate Web site - http://www.creditscoring.com - nonetheless provides numerous links related to the whys and wherefores of credit scores. After trying without much success to discover just how credit scores are calculated and used, I found I kept hearing the theme to "Mission Impossible" playing in my head while voice spoke from a tape recorder, "Your mission, should you choose to accept it, is to discover how a credit score is calculated and what minimum score is required to qualify for a Fannie Mae mortgage. Good luck. This tape will self-destruct in 5 seconds."

2. Remember this question from Chapter 12? Let's do the exercise again. This time, you'll know what duration gap is. Return to the introductory Web page for Fannie Mae - http://www.fanniemae.com. Click on "Stockholders" from the "Investors" menu at the left margin of the page. Click on "Monthly Disclosure of Interest Rate Risk, Credit Risk, Risk-Based Capital, and Liquidity, [Month, Day, Year]" near the bottom of the page. Has the effective duration gap for Fannie Mae been mostly positive or generally negative?

22

Forward, Futures, and Options Agreements

SUMMARY

1. The essence of a forward contract is "price now, delivery later." Forward contracts allow the buyer (the long) and the seller (the short) to fix a price for goods to be exchanged at a later date. For example, a U.S. firm that anticipates receiving Swiss francs in six months might agree to sell Swiss francs for dollars in six months at an exchange rate of 0.60 dollars to one Swiss franc. The U.S firm is afraid that the Swiss franc will fall in value relative to the dollar (the francs they anticipate receiving will buy fewer U.S. dollars). In six months, if the exchange rate is below 0.60 (the dollar has appreciated), the reduced dollar value of the Swiss francs the firm receives will be at least partially offset by the increase in value of the forward contract. However, if the Swiss franc appreciates, the firm will lose money on its forward contract that offsets the increased dollar value of the francs the firm receives. Perhaps a simpler way to view the issue is to say that the firm has "locked in" an exchange rate of 0.60.

2. Futures contracts are similar to forward contracts. However, futures contracts are standardized, which gives them greater liquidity allowing them to be traded on exchanges. Futures contracts also involve a clearinghouse. The clearinghouse guarantees execution of the futures contracts. This eliminates counterparty risk, the risk that the opposite party will default on his or her obligations, provided, of course, that the clearinghouse itself does not fail. To protect itself, the clearinghouse requires both side of the futures contract to post performance bonds. These performance bonds are known as margin, an unfortunate and confusing second use of the term margin, as these performance bonds are not in any sense loans used to buy additional securities. If a party to the futures contracts defaults, the clearinghouse keeps the performance bond. Furthermore, futures contracts are "marked-to-market." This means that at the end of each trading day the losing side of the contract must post additional cash to the clearinghouse (called variation margin). Margin and marking-to-market are tools that allow the clearinghouse to manage its exposure to default risk.

3. Futures prices reflect supply and demand conditions. They also reflect peoples' expectations as to future conditions. Finally, futures prices reflect what are known as "carrying costs." For example, if supply and demand results in a current price of $100 for a unit of a commodity and if it costs $10 per unit to "carry" the commodity to the future delivery date, then the price of the futures contract for the commodity, for that delivery date, should be $110. If the futures price is higher than $110, arbitrageurs will buy the spot commodity and sell the future, locking in a risk-free return. If the futures price is below $110, arbitrageurs will sell the spot commodity and buy the future and, again, lock in a risk-free return. Unfortunately, the real world is rather more complicated than my simple example and arbitrage can't always be relied on to keep spot and futures prices in line, but it's the place to start in seeking to answer the question, "How are futures prices determined?"

4. A call is the right, but not the obligation, to buy a specified good (say, 100 shares of IBM common stock) at a stated price (called the exercise price; also called the strike price) on (if the option is a "European" option) or before (if the option is an "American" option) a stated date (called the expiration date). A put is the right, but not the obligation, to sell a specified good (say, 100 shares of IBM common stock) at a stated price (called the exercise price; also called the strike price) on (if the option is a "European" option) or before (if the option is an "American" option) a stated date (called the expiration date). The purchaser of an option is called the buyer; the opposite party is called the writer. The writer agrees to be bound by the contract. The call writer must sell if the call buyer exercises his or her right to buy, the put writer must buy if the put buyer exercises his or her right to sell. In exchange for agreeing to these terms, the option writer receives a payment (the option premium). Call buyers profit if prices rise, put buyers profit if prices fall. Options are often more attractive instruments to use in hedging risks as the option buyer may choose to not exercise (i.e., to not sell or to not buy) if such exercise is unattractive. So the U.S. firm that expects to receive Swiss francs in six months might enter into a put giving it the right to sell Swiss franc for dollars in six months. If the franc falls in value, the firm exercises its right and sells the franc at the higher strike price. If, however, the franc appreciates, the firm chooses to not exercise, simply letting the put expire. The firm can still benefit from appreciation of the Swiss franc (i.e., it is not "locked in" as was the case by using futures or forward contracts). However, this greater flexibility of options is not free. The option premium must be paid up front, rather like insurance premiums must be paid prior to insurance coverage coming into effect.

5. Calls are more valuable (sell for a higher premium) when the price of the commodity rises. A call with a lower strike is more valuable than a call with a higher strike price. A call is more valuable (generally) when the expiration date is further away. A call is more valuable if the volatility of the underlying commodity is higher (higher probability that the price of the commodity will move above the strike price of the call). Puts are more valuable (sell for a higher premium) when the price of the commodity falls. A put with a higher strike is more valuable than a put with a lower strike price. A put is more valuable (generally) when the expiration date is further away. A put is more valuable if the volatility of the underlying commodity is higher (higher probability that the price of the commodity will move below the strike price of the put).

TRUE/FALSE QUESTIONS

T F 1. Both forward contracts and futures contracts involve a clearinghouse and the use of performance bonds (margin).

T F 2. If the spot (i.e., immediate delivery) price is $65 and the relevant cost of carry is $3, a futures price of $62 indicates that an arbitrage is available.

T F 3. Currency exchange forward contracts are more widely used than are currency exchange futures contracts.

T F 4. A U.S corporation has signed a contract obligating them to purchase, four months from now, a Japanese made machine tool for 100,000,000 yen. To hedge their exposure to changes in the rate of exchange between dollars and yen, the U.S. corporation should enter into a forward contract to buy yen.

Chapter 22　　　　　　　　　　　　　　　　　　　　　　　Forward, Futures, and Options Agreements

T F　　5.　At initiation, forward contracts have zero value (i.e., neither the long nor the short makes an upfront payment to enter into the contract).

T F　　6.　Because they are standardized contracts, futures contracts have greater liquidity than forward contracts have.

T F　　7.　Actual delivery of the commodity is rarely made under most futures contracts.

T F　　8.　Both the long and the short are obligated to take or make delivery under a futures contract.

T F　　9.　In options contracts, only the writer of the option is obligated, either to take delivery, for a put, or make delivery, for a call.

T F　　10.　Forward, futures, and options all may be used to hedge, but only forward and futures contracts are used to speculate.

T F　　11.　Option contracts are marked-to-market at the end of each trading day with the losing side required to post additional cash known as variation margin.

T F　　12.　A U.S corporation has signed a contract obligating them to purchase, four months from now, a Japanese made machine tool for 100,000,000 yen. To hedge their exposure to changes in the rate of exchange between dollars and yen, the U.S. corporation could buy a call on yen.

T F　　13.　Put buyers make money when the price of the asset underlying the put falls.

T F　　14.　The only reward to option writers is the premium they receive for entering into the contract.

T F　　15.　Forward contracts, futures, and options are all types of derivatives.

T F　　16.　A call with a higher strike price is more valuable than a call with a lower strike price, all else held equal.

T F　　17.　In general, the longer the time to expiration, the more valuable is the call.

T F　　18.　In general, options on very risky assets will be worth less than options on less risky assets.

T F　　19.　A speculator who believes that the dollar will soon appreciate against the yen, would want to buy a put on the yen (i.e., would want to have the option to sell yen to the writer of the option at the strike price of the put).

T F　　20.　As the expiration date of a forward or futures contracts nears, the spot price and the forward/futures price must get closer and closer to one another.

MULTIPLE CHOICE QUESTIONS

1. Which of the following is clearly an arbitrage?
   a. The spot price is $100, carry costs are $10, and the futures price is $110.
   b. The spot price is $100, carry costs are $10, and the forward price is $110.
   c. The spot price is $78 the strike price of the put is $75, and the put premium is $5.
   d. The spot price is $75, carry costs are $4, and the forward price is $80.

2. If the current exchange rate is 1.00 mark costs $0.45 and the six months forward exchange rate is 1.00 mark costs $0.50:
   a. the dollar is expected to appreciate against the mark
   b. carry costs of the contract must exceed $0.05 per mark
   c. an arbitrage is clearly available
   d. the dollar is expected to depreciate against the mark

3. A farmer is worried that the price he will receive for his corn will fall. To hedge this risk:
   a. he should start growing wheat
   b. he should go long a corn futures contract
   c. he should buy a put on corn
   d. he should buy a call on corn

4. Most dealers in currency exchange forward contracts are:
   a. commercial banks
   b. GSEs
   c. wealthy individuals
   d. credit unions

5. Futures contracts exist on all of the following except:
   a. Treasury bonds
   b. stock indexes
   c. foreign currencies
   d. automobile receivables

6. One can hedge using:
   a. calls
   b. futures
   c. puts
   d. all of the above

7. At initiation of a futures contract, the futures price is $2.25 per bushel of wheat. At expiration of the futures contract, the price is $1.95 per bushel of wheat.
   a. the long profited by $0.30 per bushel
   b. the short profited by $0.30 per bushel
   c. more information is needed before we can determine if the long or the short profited from the price move
   d. demand for wheat has risen relative to its supply

8. Price this forward contract. The spot price of the commodity is $2.00, carry cost is equal to 5% per year, and there is exactly one-year until delivery.
   a. $2.20
   b. $2.10
   c. $2.05
   d. $2.00

9. Futures differ from forward contracts in that:
   a. futures have more counterparty risk (default risk) than do forward contracts
   b. futures are marked-to-market and forward contracts are not
   c. futures prices are based on the cost of carry but forward prices are not
   d. futures involve delivery at a future time but forward contracts do not

10. A call option would have a higher premium if:
    a. it had a higher strike price than another call
    b. stock prices fall
    c. it is exercised
    d. the time to expiration is longer

11. Arbitrageurs are best characterized as:
    a. uninformed
    b. long-term investors
    c. gamblers
    d. none of the above

12. When prices fall:
    a. shorts profit
    b. put buyers profit
    c. call writers avoid losses
    d. all of the above
    e. none of the above

13. Put writers hope prices:
    a. rise
    b. stay the same
    c. fall
    d. either a or b

14. Options on futures:
    a. don't exist
    b. become futures contracts if exercised
    c. have no expiration date
    d. have no strike price

15. In order to protect an investment in Treasury bonds from rising interest rates:
    a. one would buy a put on Treasury bonds
    b. one would go long Treasury bond futures
    c. one would sell a put on Treasury bond futures
    d. one would use margin to leverage the investment in Treasury bonds

FILL IN QUESTIONS

1. A _____ is the right to sell.

2. If you short a futures contract, you agree to _____ the commodity at expiration.

3. To offset a long (bought) call, one would _____ a _____ with the same strike, expiration date, and for the same asset.

4. Futures contracts are _____, but forward contracts can be _____ to meet the specific needs of a customer.

5. A speculator who believes that interest rates are about to fall would _____ a Treasury bond futures contract.

6. Both the buyer and the seller in futures contracts must post performance bonds called _____ at the initiation of the contract.

7. A call with a strike price of $40 would be worth _____ than a call with a strike price of $45, holding all other factors constant.

8. The most active options exchange is located in _____.

9. _____ writers have an obligation to buy, if the option is exercised against them.

10. The price of an option is most often referred to as the option's _____.

ESSAY QUESTIONS and INTERNET EXERCISES

1. The Chicago Mercantile Exchange categorizes the factors that affect currency trading into three sets of factors. Navigate the CME Web site - http://www.cme.com - until you find the factors. Write the factors down and then associate each factor with the chapter in the text that discusses that factor.

2. Many currency options trade on the Philadelphia Exchange. Go to the PHLX Web site - http://www.phlx.com - and look through the PHLX products until you find the currencies that options trade on. How many such currencies are there? Are these option American style options or European style options (careful, there's a trick to this question)?

23

Asset-Backed Securities, Interest-Rate Agreements, and Currency Swaps

SUMMARY

1. One of the most important developments in finance in recent years is securitization. Securitization can turn relatively illiquid, unattractive investments such as mortgages into more attractive subsets of securities (called "tranches," which is French for slices). Mortgages and similar investments are unattractive because when interest rates rise, the prices of mortgages fall, but when interest rates fall, borrowers pay off their mortgages early, forcing investors to reinvest at the new, lower rates. Understanding prepayment risk is essential to understanding the risk of investing in mortgages and the advantages securitization brings.

2. There are five steps to a securitization:

    (1) Borrowers take out a loan (for example, a 30-year fixed rate mortgage).

    (2) The lender pools similar loans and sells the pool of loans to a trust (using a trust has important tax implications as it allows the mortgage payments to be passed through to the eventual bondholders without income taxes being imposed on the trust).

    (3) The trusts intend to issue bonds with the pool of loans acting as collateral. The trusts, therefore, have the about to be issued bonds rated by S&P or Moody's.

    (4) If needed, the trust seeks a "credit enhancer" such as a guarantee of repayment from an insurance company.

    (5) An underwriter takes the bonds to the public or places them privately.

3. The bonds issued using the pool of loans as collateral can have various characteristics. One of the most common approaches is to establish tranches such that the "A" tranche will receive all prepayments up to a stated notional amount. Then tranche "B" receives the prepayments, then "C," and so on. Tranche "Z" (for zero coupon) might be a residual tranche, which receives payments only after the other tranches are paid off. Tranche "A" effectively becomes a short-term bond, "B" and "C" are intermediate term, while "Z" is long-term, zero coupon bond. Each of these types of

investments might be attractive to particular investors, investors who would not find the mortgages themselves to be attractive investments. Done well, the parts (the tranches) will sell for more than the whole (the underlying loans), making a nice profit for the party that put the pool together.

4. Securitization increases the funds available for the type of lending that generates the collateral. For example, securitization has increased the availability of mortgages. Securitization reduces the cost of the loans (e.g., mortgage rates are lower than they would otherwise be). Customized tranches can be created to precisely match an investor's needs. On the other hand, loan decisions are more and more made on the basis of whether or not the loan will be eligible for securitization. This means that the securitization rules (credit scoring, etc.) become dominant. Almost any dependable stream of revenue has the potential to be securitized. For example, royalties from the sale of record albums by David Bowie have been securitized.

5. Interest rate swaps allow parties to trade interest payment streams. Although the number of types of swaps continues to grow and they have become ever more exotic, explanation of a "plain vanilla" interest rate swap will do for this text. Suppose one bank has made a fixed rate loan, but now wishes it could receive floating rate payments (perhaps because it expects interest rates to go up). Another bank wants to change its floating rate loan into a fixed rate (can you think of reason why?). The banks might agree to a swap. The first bank would agree to pay the second bank the fixed payments it receives from its borrower in exchange for the floating payments of the second bank. The second bank would agree to send its floating payments to the first bank in exchange for the first bank's fixed payments. The banks would negotiate a spread (an additional amount to be added or subtracted to one of the streams), a term for the swap, and a notional principal. Say the notional principal was $100,000, the fixed rate is 7%, the floating rate is LIBOR, the spread is 50 BP added to LIBOR, and the term of the swap is one year. For simplicity, assume the swap payments are annual, rather than the typical quarterly swap payments. Assume LIBOR for the swap period turns out to be 3.25%. At the end of the year the first bank would owe $7,000 to the second bank, the second bank would owe $3,750 to the first (LIBOR plus 50 BP). Only the difference, $3,250 would actually be exchanged. Note that the notional principal of $100,000 was not exchanged at the initiation of the swap (explaining why it is only a notional principal, not a real payment).

6. An interest rate cap is an agreement in which the writer of the cap, in exchange for a premium, agrees to compensate the buyer of the cap if interest rates rise above a stated level (the strike rate). An interest rate floor is an agreement in which the writer of the cap, in exchange for a premium, agrees to compensate the buyer of the floor if interest rates fall below a stated level (the strike rate). Banks and other entities that are exposed to losses if interest rates rise might use caps as a risk management tool. Who would be willing to write caps? What sort of interest expectations would a cap writer have? Who might be eager to buy a floor? And who would write a floor? If you simultaneously buy a cap and write a floor, then you have an interest rate collar. A collar "locks in" an interest rate range. The bank protects itself from rising rates (the cap), but foregoes the benefits of lower rates (by writing the floor). The premium received on the floor reduces, in effect, the cost of the cap. Artful selection of the cap and floor features might result in the cap premium being equal to the floor premium, resulting in a zero cost collar.

7. Currency swaps are similar to interest rate swaps, with the payments made and received by the two parties being denominated in different currencies. In currency swaps, the initial principal typically is actually exchanged (i.e., it is no longer merely a notional principal). Currency swaps are another tool available to banks and other financial institutions for managing exchange rate risk. Currency swaps can be written for longer terms than is typical in the currency forward markets.

Chapter 23 — Asset-Backed Securities, Interest-Rate Agreements, and Currency Swaps

TRUE/FALSE QUESTIONS

T F 1. An interest rate cap provides the buyer of the cap with protection from falling interest rates.

T F 2. Securitization works best with those underlying assets that have a steady stream of cash flows.

T F 3. When interest rates rise, prepayments on fixed rate mortgages also increase.

T F 4. One mechanism for ensuring that the bonds issued under a securitization are highly rated is to overcollateralize the bonds. Thus, $100 million of bonds might be backed up by $120 million of pooled loans.

T F 5. Slicing the pool of underlying loans into tranches allows for the possibility that the prices received in selling the tranches exceeds the cost of the underlying pool of loans.

T F 6. Securitization has kept mortgage rates higher than they otherwise would be, allowing mortgage lenders to earn greater profits.

T F 7. Securitization has reduced the liquidity risk faced by banks and other mortgage originators.

T F 8. Interest rate swaps allow an investor to switch a fixed rate investment into a floating rate investment.

T F 9. Interest rate swaps allow an investor to switch a floating rate investment into a fixed rate investment.

T F 10. The notional principal in an interest rate swap is not actually exchanged.

T F 11. An investor that would suffer a loss if interest rates fell would be more likely to buy an interest rate floor than an interest rate cap.

T F 12. Securitization results in the creation of asset-backed securities (ABS).

T F 13. Through securitization, a pool of thirty-year mortgages can effectively be sliced into subsets of securities, some with very short-term maturities.

T F 14. In general, asset-backed securities are more liquid than their underlying collateral.

T F 15. The only reward from writing either a floor or a cap is the premium received.

MULTIPLE CHOICE QUESTIONS

1. Suppose a bank has a negative income gap (see Chapter 21). To reduce its interest rate risk, such a bank would be most likely to:
   a. write an interest rate cap
   b. buy an interest rate floor
   c. buy an interest rate cap
   d. buy a call on a Treasury bond futures contract

2. Which of the following have been successfully securitized?
   a. student loans
   b. credit card receivables
   c. automobile loans
   d. lottery winnings
   e. all of the above

3. The use of securitization has allowed banks:
   a. to reduce their excess reserves
   b. to completely eliminate interest rate risk
   c. to generally increase interest rates on the loans they make
   d. to fire their underwriters

4. A U.S. based corporation anticipates receiving a series of payments denominated in British pounds over the next ten years. To manage the exchange rate risk of this stream of payments, the corporation would most likely enter into a/an:
   a. forward contract
   b. currency swap
   c. interest rate cap
   d. interest rate floor

5. Which of the following is most similar to buying a series of puts on Treasury bonds?
   a. going long a futures contract
   b. entering into a currency swap
   c. buying an interest rate cap
   d. buying an interest rate floor

6. Typically, in interest rate swaps, the notional principal is:
   a. not disclosed
   b. not known
   c. not exchanged
   d. not denominated in monetary units

7. Securitization allows:
   a. multiple asset classes to be backed by the same underlying pool of loans
   b. specialized securities to be designed for a specific investor
   c. lenders to reduce their cost of funds
   d. all of the above

8. One nice feature of asset-backed securities is:
   a. they have no default risk
   b. they allow banks the freedom to pick and choose loans based primarily on criteria of the bank's own design
   c. they are inexpensive to package and market
   d. none of the above

9. The buyer of an interest rate cap receives payments when:
   a. interest rates rise
   b. interest rates fall
   c. interest rates rise above the stated strike rate
   d. interest rates become more volatile

10. If interest rates stay below the strike rate for the duration of an interest rate cap, the buyer of the cap receives:
    a. nothing
    b. the premium
    c. the difference between the average interest rate over the period and the strike rate
    d. an interest rate floor

FILL IN QUESTIONS

1. Given that the underwriter that brings asset-backed securities to the market generally then makes-a-market in those securities, ABSs tend to have greater _____ than the assets underlying them.

2. The various 'slices" that a pool of mortgages can be effectively divided into in a securitization are known as _____.

3. Sallie Mae plays an important role in the securitization of _____.

4. An interest rate collar is a combination of a _____ and a _____.

5. A bank wishing to change a fixed rate asset into a floating rate asset would use a _____ to accomplish the task.

6. Suppose a bank buys an interest rate cap and writes an interest rate floor. If interest rate subsequently fall below the strike price on the floor, the bank will _____ payments _____ the buyer of the floor.

7. In general, only _____ payments are exchanged in an interest rate swap.

8. Currency swaps involve at least _____ currencies.

9. Suppose a bank has entered into an interest rate swap and has agreed to pay the fixed rate and receive the floating rate. To protect itself from losses due to changes in the floating rate, the bank might next buy an interest rate _____.

10. Currency swaps often cover a _____ time period than forward contracts on currencies.

ESSAY QUESTIONS and INTERNET EXERCISES

1. The International Swaps and Derivatives Association Web site - http://www.isda.org - has links to numerous sites related to derivatives, risk management, and swaps. Click on "Who We Are" and write out a summary of the mission statement of the ISDA. Then try "Educational Information" and click on "Useful Links" under the "Educational Information" menu. Read the article by Thomas F. Siems and answer these questions: (1) What type and level of regulation does Mr. Siems argue is appropriate for derivatives? (2) What are the "ten myths" of derivatives?

2. The Global Association of Risk Professionals (GARP) sponsors the Financial Risk Manager (FRM) professional designation. Search the GARP Web site at - http://www.garp.com - to learn more about the FRM certificate. Write down the certification requirements one needs to achieve to earn the FRM certificate. How much does it cost to sit for the FRM exam?

24

Monetary Policy and the Financial System

SUMMARY

1. The goals of monetary policy are two: sustainable economic growth and price stability.

    a. Sustainable economic growth means economic growth that proceeds along the long-term trend. Deviations around the trend line are relatively small, neither too high (a booming economy) nor too small (a recession). Of course, booms and busts have occurred and likely will occur again, but the goal remains the same – to attenuate deviations and return to the long-term growth trend. Real GDP growth in the range of 2.5% to 3% per year appears to be consistent with sustainable growth in the U.S.

    b. Price stability means that the economy experiences neither inflation (generally rising prices) nor deflation (falling prices). Some also worry about disinflation, which occurs when the rate of inflation falls, especially when it falls below the rate they believe is consistent with sustainable economic growth (i.e., such economists believe that a little inflation is a good thing). Changing prices affect the economy the way severe static affects radio or telephone communication. It is difficult for economic actors to send consistent or useful price messages when prices are changing. Does an increase in price mean that demand for an item increased and we should expand production, or is it just a consequence of inflation?

    c. The Employment Act of 1944 and the Humphrey-Hawkins Full Employment and Balanced Growth Act of 1978 are the two major pieces of federal legislation affecting monetary policy. In attempting to meet the often conflicting goals of these laws (price stability and sustainable growth), policy makers have used the unemployment rate as a summary measure. Some economists believe there is a consistent relationship between inflation, unemployment, and economic growth, a concept crystallized in the "non-accelerating inflation rate of unemployment" (NAIRU) statistic. NAIRU of approximately 4% to 4.5% was their goal, although much of the 1990s saw unemployment below 4% without significant inflation.

2. Economists working for the Federal Reserve System analyze a multitude of data relating to the economy. Their goal is to advise the Board of Governors as to when monetary policy should be tightened and when loosened. The job is a difficult one. First, the economists and policymakers face a recognition lag. That is, some time elapses between changes in the economy and the recognition of those changes by the statisticians. Next, there is a policy lag, which is the time between recognition that an economic problem is developing and the designing of policies to alleviate the problem. Finally, there is the impact lag, the time between implementation of the policy and observing actual changes in inflation, unemployment, and growth. Furthermore, all three lags are

quite variable. All this leads to the observation that monetary policy is about equal parts guesswork and data analysis. In response to these lags, and the variation in the lags, the Fed uses intermediate targets to guide its day-to-day operations. I think of these intermediate targets as the lines near the top of a bowling alley. Instead of focusing on the distant pins, bowlers use these lines to guide the placement of the ball. If you place the ball within the proper lines at the top of the lane, you'll knock over the pins at the end of the lane. The intermediate targets used by the Fed have included M1 growth, M2 growth, changes in DNFD, and the Fed funds rate. As the relationships between these intermediate targets and inflation and growth have changed over the years, the Fed has substituted one intermediate target for another and adjusted the target values.

3. The FOMC meets and, despite all the difficulties discussed above, decides that monetary conditions should be changed. To effect the decision, they send what's known as a policy directive to the trading desk of the New York Federal Reserve Bank. The directive might state, in part, "… the Committee seeks conditions in the reserve markets consistent with reducing the federal funds rate to 2.5%." This provides the essential guidance to the trading desk – supply reserve to the banking system until Fed funds fall to about 2.5%. After analyzing bank reserves and establishing a first guess as to the reserves needed to be consistent with the Fed funds target, the trading desk begins to buy (in this example) Treasury bills from the public. How would the trading desk execute a policy directive to increase the Fed funds rate?

TRUE/FALSE QUESTIONS

T F 1. Of the tools of monetary policy available to the Federal Reserve, the most important is open market operations.

T F 2. Sustainable economic growth is output growth above the economy's long-term growth path.

T F 3. Price stability means inflation so low and stable that it is ignored by households and firms in making economic choices.

T F 4. For purposes of monetary policy, the size of the economy is typically measured by nominal GDP.

T F 5. Unemployment means slower economic growth because some resources (i.e., potential workers) are being wasted.

T F 6. A stable economic environment allows firms to be more farsighted in their financial and production decision-making.

T F 7. Output that could have been produced last year by those who were unemployed is lost forever and can never be made up.

T F 8. Inflation redistributes income in arbitrary and unpredictable ways from workers to firms and from lenders to borrowers.

T F 9. Households pay proportionately more taxes to government in an inflationary environment.

T F 10. U.S. income taxes are based on real rates of return, not nominal returns.

T F 11. The natural rate of unemployment is defined as the rate of unemployment that would occur in the absence of government intervention.

T F 12. Economic growth beyond 2% per year does not seem to be sustainable over the long-term.

T F 13. It typically takes several months, at a minimum, before the consequences of implementing a monetary policy appear in the economy.

T F 14. The various economic indicators used by the Fed to guide monetary policy often give contradictory signals regarding economic growth or price stability.

T F 15. The policy lag is the time between the recognition that action is needed and the time that the appropriate policy is set into motion.

MULTIPLE CHOICE QUESTIONS

1. Primary tools of monetary policy available to the Federal Reserve include:
   a. changes in the discount rate
   b. changes in the required reserve ratio
   c. open market operations
   d. all of the above

2. The objectives of monetary policy include:
   a. world peace
   b. sustainable economic growth
   c. disinflation
   d. a profitable commercial banking community
   e. b and d

3. Productivity of labor depends on:
   a. the capital stock with which they work
   b. the health of the workforce
   c. education
   d. all of the above

4. The most frequently used measure of inflation is:
   a. the consumer price index (CPI)
   b. the producer price index (PPI)
   c. the inflation price index (IPI)
   d. the Goldman-Sachs commodity price index

5. Which of the following is most damaging to economic performance?
   a. expected inflation
   b. unexpected inflation
   c. improbable inflation
   d. impossible inflation

6. All of the following increase the difficulty of conducting monetary policy except:
   a. policy lag
   b. recognition lag
   c. implementation lag
   d. impact lag

7. The impact lag is defined as:
   a. the time between recognition that policy must be changed and actually issuing the new policy directive
   b. the time between when corrective action is taken and when that action has an impact on prices, unemployment, or output
   c. the randomness in the series of data used to guide monetary policy
   d. the time it takes to study the data and recognize that a problem is developing.
   e. none of the above

8. In implementing monetary policy, U.S. policymakers tend to be:
   a. cautious
   b. aggressive
   c. slothful
   d. ill-informed

9. Over the past twenty years, day-to-day FOMC operations have made use of intermediate targets such as:
   a. the Federal funds rate
   b. the level of M1
   c. the level of DNFD
   d. all of the above

10. Actual open market operations are carried out by:
    a. the trading desk of the FOMC
    b. the trading desk of Merrill Lynch
    c. the trading desk of the New York Times
    d. the trading desk of the Federal Reserve Bank of New York

FILL IN QUESTIONS

1. The two goals of monetary policy are _____ and _____.

2. Policies that achieve _____ and a noninflationary environment in the short run help to achieve sustainable growth and _____ in the long run.

3. The more important of the two monetary goals (or, more simply, the primary goal of monetary policy) is usually considered to be _____.

4. Over the past ten years or so, due to the increasingly global impact of sophisticated communications, as well as for other reasons, central bankers have seen their ability to control economic behavior _____.

5. Since mid-1993, the Fed has emphasized _____ as its intermediate target.

6. Privately created mechanisms for making payments over the Internet have come to be known as _____.

7. The document that communicates the FOMC instructions to the trading desk is the _____.

8. To ease monetary conditions, the trading desk will _____ Treasury bills.

9. _____ automatically move money at the end of each day from accounts that are subject to reserve requirements and into deposits that are not subject to reserve requirements.

10. The three lags that affect monetary policy are _____, _____, and _____.

ESSAY QUESTIONS and INTERNET EXERCISES

1. Go to the Federal Open Market Committee Web site at - http://www.federalreserve.gov/FOMC. Click on "Meetings calendar, statements, and minutes ." Read the latest policy statement. Is the Fed loosening monetary policy, tightening monetary policy, or being neutral? Why?

2. Go to the Shadow Open Market Committee Web site - http://www.somc.rochester.edu. Who or what is the shadow open market committee? Click on the "Policy Statement" link near the bottom of the opening page. Does the SOMC recommend loosening monetary policy, tightening monetary policy, or being neutral? Why?

25

Monetary Policy in a Globalized Financial System

SUMMARY

1. Monetary policy under fixed exchange rates – the Bretton Woods Accord. The fixed exchange rate system that was in place from 1944 until 1973 had certain "natural" feedback elements to it that made inflation and unemployment self-correcting. If a country experienced higher inflation, its balance of payments would fall as its (high priced) exports fell. Capital would flow out of the country. The high inflation country would be forced, under the Bretton Woods Accord, to buy back its currency, reducing its money supply, and, thus, reducing inflation. If unemployment in a country increased, income would fall and so would imports. The balance of payments would move to a surplus increasing the country's reserves. The increased reserves would lead to an increase in the domestic money supply, sparking economic growth, and solving the unemployment problem. Despite these apparent self-correcting controls, the fixed exchange rate system eventually failed. The failure was due to the unwillingness of countries to yield control over their domestic economies to the need to support their currencies. Countries would resist changing their monetary policy until a crisis forced them to change. Instead of smooth feedback control, the world experienced a series of devaluations and revaluations that proved to be destabilizing and eventually unsustainable.

2. Monetary policy under flexible exchange rates. Currency exchange rates now adjust rapidly to supply and demand conditions. Now, should authorities seek to expand the domestic economy with the attendant balance of trade deficit, currency markets and capital flows will respond quickly, reducing the impact of the domestic monetary stimulus. Attempts to slow a domestic economy would also be partially offset by immediate responses in the capital and currency markets. To a greater and greater extent, monetary policy, to be effective, must be coordinated across national boundaries (actually and more specifically, across *currency* boundaries).

3. Dollarization is an interesting approach to managing monetary problems. Despite its name, it does not relate just to the U.S. dollar, although the dollar is often used in such schemes. Dollarization occurs when a country uses another country's currency as its own. For example, the currency of Panama is the U.S. dollar. As the dollar is considered to be a stable currency, Panama reaps the benefits of reduced volatility. Dollarization requires the country accepting another country's currency as its own to forego seigniorage. Seigniorage is the difference between the cost of producing and distributing currency and any revenues earned through the distribution. For example, it costs pennies to print a $50, bill but the Treasury/Federal Reserve recognizes $50 of value on that "investment" of a few pennies. A currency board also has a nation base its currency on

the value of another nation's currency, but it does not actually replace its currency. Generally, the currency board fixes the exchange rate of the local currency vis-à-vis the outside currency. For example, until recently, Argentina fixed the value of its peso at one-to-one with the U.S. dollar.

TRUE/FALSE QUESTIONS

T F 1. Under the fixed exchange rate system established by the Bretton Woods Accord, inflation and unemployment problems were self-correcting, provided that the countries involved fulfilled their obligations to buy or sell their currencies as obligated by the accord.

T F 2. Under fixed exchange rates, exchange rate risk was minimized (at least in the near-term).

T F 3. Discrete, relatively large reductions in the value of a nation's currency relative to other currencies are known as revaluations.

T F 4. When market participants supply more of a currency to the currency market, the value of that currency will fall.

T F 5. The world currently operates under a flexible exchange rate system.

T F 6. International trade and capital flows have increased dramatically over the past thirty years.

T F 7. Seigniorage is the difference between the cost of producing and distributing currency and the revenue earned by the distribution.

T F 9. Under dollarization schemes involving the U.S. dollar, seigniorage for the United States government is increased.

T F 10. Dollarization schemes are generally implemented using currency boards.

T F 11. Under floating exchange rates, monetary authorities have actually intervened more often in the currency markets than was the case under fixed rates.

T F 12. An example of sterilization would be if the Fed supplied dollars to the currency markets, but then removed an equivalent amount of dollars from domestic reserves.

T F 13. Under the new Eurosystem the Federal Reserve Board of Governors will conduct the monetary policies of the European Union.

T F 14. Fixed exchange rates can only be sustained over the long-term if the growth and inflation rates of the participating countries are similar.

T F 15. The future will require countries to coordinate their monetary policies regardless of whether exchange rates are fixed or flexible.

MULTIPLE CHOICE QUESTIONS

1. When the money supply is increased:
   a. short-term interest rates are likely to fall
   b. long-term interest rates might rise if the increase kicks off fear of increased inflation
   c. short-term interest rates are likely to increase
   d. a and b

2. Under the terms of the Bretton Woods Accord, imbalance in current and capital accounts could persist if:
   a. countries experienced different growth rates
   b. countries experienced different inflation rates
   c. countries' had different term structures of interest rates
   d. any or all of the above

3. Under fixed exchange rates, at least in theory,
   a. inflation and unemployment are positively related
   b. the rate of inflation always exceed the rate of unemployment
   c. the rate of inflation is always less than the rate of unemployment
   d. inflation and unemployment problems are self-correcting

4. Which of following involve discrete changes in the official exchange rate?
   a. devaluation
   b. revaluation
   c. subsequentiation
   d. a and b
   e. all of the above

5. If the fear of a devaluation drives speculators to supply more of the about to be devalued currency to the currency markets:
   a. the devaluation becomes more likely
   b. the speculators are certain to lose substantial sums of money
   c. the devaluation becomes less likely
   d. the nation's central bank should counter the threat by increasing the supply of its currency to the currency market

6. Central banks are often unwilling to act until a crisis is upon them because:
   a. they are spineless
   b. the domestic consequences of their actions are often unpleasant
   c. they simply don't know what to do
   d. monetary policy is most effective in a crisis atmosphere

7. In 2000, both imports into the United States and exports from the U.S. exceeded _____ percent of Gross National Product (GNP). Choose the most correct answer.
   a. 100
   b. 30
   c. 10
   d. 2

8. To slow economic activity, the Federal Reserve might:
   a. attempt to increase interest rates
   b. allow interest rates to fall
   c. increase the corporate income tax rate
   d. close all access to the discount window

9. Countries choosing dollarization:
   a. have likely experienced high inflation rates in the recent past
   b. lose the benefits of seigniorage
   c. might tie their currencies to an index of other currencies rather than to just one currency
   d. a and b
   e. all of the above

FILL IN QUESTIONS

1. In an attempt to make its exports more competitively priced, a nation might be tempted to _____ its currency.

2. _____ are willing to accept substantial risk in an attempt to earn high rewards by entering into currency markets transactions based on their belief that a currency is either undervalued or overvalued.

3. As barriers to international trade continue to fall, central banks will find it more and more necessary to _____ monetary policy.

4. If U.S. interest rates increase, holding all other factors constant, the dollar is likely to _____.

5. To slow money growth, the FOMC would _____ Treasury bills.

6. If the Federal Reserve were to supply dollars to the currency market, but simultaneously reduce the domestic money supply by approximately the same amount, the Fed is attempting to _____ its foreign exchange transactions.

7. Currency swaps are a useful tool for managing currency exchange rate risk only under a _____ exchange rate system.

8. Under flexible exchange rates, the value of a country's currency is determined by _____ and _____.

ESSAY QUESTIONS and INTERNET EXERCISES

1. Central banks often attempt to "sterilize" their currency market operations. But is sterilization effective? After all, in this world of instant communications and electronic capital flows, can the domestic money supply be managed separately from the foreign currency markets? For insight on these issues, read Jang-Yung Lee's paper at - http://www.imf.org/external/pubs/ft/issues7. What conclusions does Lee make regarding the effectiveness of sterilization for developing countries? And for industrial countries?

2. Robert Mundell won the Nobel Prize in Economics in 1999. His home page at Columbia University is - http://www.columbia.edu/~ram15/index.html. Of particular relevance to this chapter is Dr. Mundell's paper that he delivered at Universidad del CEMA, Buenos Aires, Argentina, on April 17, 2000. Click on the "CEMA2000 Lecture" link to access this paper. Read section 5 "The Importance of Monetary Rules" and section 9 "Towards a World Currency" and answer these questions: (1) what is the difference between a fixed rate of exchange and a pegged rate? (2) was the gold standard a pegged rate or a fixed rate? (3) in Mundell's opinion, would a common world currency generate greater prosperity and improved international cooperation?

Appendix

Answers to True/False, Multiple Choice, and Fill In Questions

Chapter 1

True/False
1. F, they are DSUs
2. T
3. F, see the discussion of re-regulation in Chapter 17
4. T
5. T
6. F, the U.S. central bank is the Federal Reserve System
7. T
8. F, intermediaries enhance the efficiency of financial markets
9. F, of course funds are eventually withdrawn from pension plans, etc.
10. T
11. F, just talk to two randomly chosen economists
12. T
13. T
14. F, businesses can also be providers of funds (i.e., SSUs)
15. T
16. F, to be liquid, the asset must be able to be sold quickly without a significant price concession
17. F, creation of capital goods requires foregone consumption
18. F, interest can be paid on checkable deposits
19. F, they are the largest portion of M1 (see Chapter 2)

Multiple Choice
1. d
2. b
3. a, b and c could occur for an SSU or DSU
4. a
5. d
6. c
7. d
8. e
9. d
10. b

Fill In
1. exceeds; is less than
2. Federal Reserve System
3. trough
4. higher; lower (see Exhibit 1-7)
5. return; risk

Chapter 2

True/False

1. F, to be money, the item must meet all three tests – exchange, store of value, and unit of account
2. F, inflation can erode the value of money
3. F, most money is held as checkable deposits
4. T
5. T
6. T
7. F, higher interest rates reduce demand for money
8. T
9. F, non-U.S. credit flows have significant impact
10. F, this will tend to increase inflation
11. T
12. T
13. F, see Exhibit 2-2
14. F, M1 does not include savings and time deposits
15. F, not all U.S. entities, only the non-financial entities
16. T
17. T
18. T
19. F, they form part of M2
20. T
21. T
22. F, an increase in the required reserve ratio would tend to decrease M1, and, most likely, M2 and M3 as well
23. F, in equilibrium supply equals demand
24. T
25. F, credit cards are issued by other financial institutions as well as by banks

Multiple Choice

1. c
2. a
3. a
4. a
5. c
6. b
7. d
8. c
9. d
10. b
11. e
12. d
13. d
14. a
15. e
16. c
17. d
18. e (apologies to the vegetarians)

Fill In

1. along; of
2. means of payment; store of value; unit of account
3. barter
4. M1 and M2
5. electronic funds transfer
6. the quantity demanded of money
7. required reserve ratio
8. demand for money; demanded
9. M1; M2; DNFD
10. reduce; reduce; reduce

Chapter 3

True/False
1. F, money markets trade short-term financial assets such as T-bills, CDs, etc.
2. F, Treasury notes and bonds are capital market instruments
3. T
4. F, price now, delivery later
5. F, bid prices are less than ask prices
6. T
7. F, if liquid, no reduction in price would be needed to sell the asset quickly
8. T
9. T
10. T
11. F, the opposite is true
12. F, mortgages are capital market instruments
13. F, dealers buy and sell from inventory, brokers act as agents for their customers
14. F, munis are attractive to high income, high tax bracket investors
15. F, they are two completely separate currencies – the U.S. dollar and the new currency of much of Europe called the Euro
16. T
17. F, rather than default, the U.S. Treasury would simply create money to pay its debts
18. T
19. T
20. F, a viable secondary market is needed to entice investors to purchase securities in the primary market
21. T
22. F, both may be sold prior to maturity
23. T
24. F, they give advice, etc.
25. T

Multiple Choice
1. b
2. c
3. d
4. b
5. d
6. a
7. d
8. b
9. a
10. d
11. e
12. d
13. b
14. c

Fill In
1. thirty years
2. General obligation; revenue
3. primary; secondary
4. capital; money
5. decline
6. negotiable certificate of deposit (CD)
7. Eurodollars
8. ask bid

Chapter 4

True/False
1. T
2. F, members are appointed by the president with the advice and consent of the Senate
3. F, the banks are headquartered in their respective districts
4. F, the FOMC meets eight times a year
5. T
6. T
7. F, the Chair of the Board of Governors usually chairs the FOMC
8. F, only the New York president is a permanent member of the FOMC
9. F, minutes of a meeting are released after the subsequent meeting
10. T
11. T
12. T
13. T
14. F, they can only borrow at the discount window to meet temporary or emergency liquidity needs
15. F, lender of last resort means that in a crisis, the Fed will supply loans to banks even when no other entity will
16. T
17. F, it would increase the election pressure on the Fed
18. F, they are set by the Board of Governors
19. F, it is zero (no reserves are needed against time and savings deposits)
20. F, fed funds are loans between member banks
21. T
22. F, the Thrift Institutions Advisory Council is weak
23. F, the bank is located in San Francisco, Los Angeles has a branch
24. F, seven members are so appointed
25. F, state banks have the option to join or not join

Multiple Choice
1. d
2. d
3. b
4. b
5. b
6. d
7. a
8. c
9. c
10. d
11. d
12. d
13. d
14. e
15. e
16. a

Fill In
1. lender-of-last-resort
2. Board of Governors
3. New York
4. FOMC (Federal Open Market Committee)
5. transactions
6. privilege, not a right
7. required reserve
8. 1907
9. buy
10. scapegoat

Chapter 5

True/False
1. F, interest rates will also fall
2. T
3. T
4. T
5. F, it is selling at a discount
6. T
7. T
8. F, interest rates are likely to fall
9. F, the supply of loanable funds will increase if the savings rate increases
10. F, the Fed would reduce interest rates
11. T
12. T
13. T
14. T
15. T
16. T
17. T
18. F, to reduce the fear of inflation, the Fed would reduce the money supply
19. F, the price is equal to the present value of the cash flows
20. T
21. T
22. F, its value would be equal to the present value of the maturity payment discounted at the appropriate discount rate
23. T
24. T

Multiple Choice
1. a
2. c
3. a
4. b
5. d
6. b
7. b
8. c
9. a
10. c
11. a
12. c
13. d
14. b
15. a
16. b
17. b
18. c
19. a
20. c

Fill In
1. coupons; maturity
2. multiplying
3. dividing
4. $1,000
5. its yield to maturity (YTM)
6. discount
7. increases
8. increased
9. consol
10. rise

Chapter 6

True/False
1. F, current interest rates will increase or remain the same
2. F, higher rated bonds pay lower returns
3. F, the after-tax return on the corporate would be 5.22, which exceeds the muni's return
4. T
5. T
6. F, the yield curve is the graphical depiction of the term structure of interest rates
7. T
8. F, don't subtract one, add one
9. F, rates are more likely to rise as economic growth picks up
10. T
11. T
12. F, see T/F question 13
13. T
14. T
15. F, AAA is the highest rating
16. F, the expected one year rate one year from now is 6.50%
17. F, a downward sloping yield curve can be consistent with the liquidity premium theory if expected future rates are low enough
18. F, munis can default
19. T
20. T

Multiple Choice
1. b
2. a
3. b
4. a
5. a
6. d
7. b
8. d
9. c
10. b
11. a
12. d
13. c
14. a
15. c
16. d
17. b
18. c
19. a

Fill In
1. yield curve
2. geometric
3. more
4. little
5. segmented markets
6. upwards
7. Moody's and Standard & Poor's
8. the yield to maturity (YTM)
9. zero
10. expectations

Chapter 7

True/False
1. F, expectations are key
2. F, it impossible to consistently earn excess risk-adjusted returns
3. T
4. T
5. T
6. T
7. T
8. F, rational expectations incorporates evaluation of future possibilities, adaptive expectations does not
9. T
10. F, insider information, by definition, is not "readily available"
11. T
12. F, only a few investors need to possess this information for these informed investors to drive prices to an efficient outcome
13. T
14. F, it is not impossible to make predictions, some things are quite predictable, I predict it will be warmer this January in Singapore than it will be in Greenland
15. F, how can you currently learn from a mistake that not yet happened?
16. F, the best forecast is the security's expected price
17. T
18. F, they will be zero on average, not zero every time
19. T
20. T
21. T
22. F, borrowing must equal lending for the entire economy, but not necessarily for each sector

Multiple Choice
1. a
2. c
3. e
4. b
5. d
6. d
7. d
8. a
9. b
10. d
11. a
12. c
13. d
14. b
15. c
16. e
17. a
18. e
19. e
20. a

Fill In
1. Rational
2. increasing
3. information
4. more recently
5. interest rates
6. sources
7. lending
8. households; government; non-financial businesses; non-U.S.
9. equilibrium
10. expected; forecast

Chapter 8

True/False
1. T
2. F, prices will be equal after adjusting for the exchange rates
3. F, the dollar is likely to depreciate
4. F, the dollar/yen rate is 0.007813
5. F, look at recent U.S. history
6. F, by definition, these accounts must balance, you can't have simultaneous surpluses
7. F, demand for dollars will increase as U.S. goods will appear to cost less in Japan
8. F, the dollar is more likely to fall
9. F, one Swiss Franc costs 5.61 pesos
10. F, the supply of dollars will fall (Mexican goods will appear to be more expensive to U.S. consumers)
11. T
12. T
13. T
14. F, high inflation in the U.S. will cause the dollar to fall in value
15. T
16. F, remember, the capital account is in surplus
17. F, the Canadian dollar will increase in value
18. T
19. F, the dollar will fall in value
20. F, if you wait, the Toyota will cost more in dollar terms
21. T

Multiple Choice
1. c
2. b
3. a
4. d
5. c
6. c
7. b
8. b
9. b
10. a
11. b
12. a
13. c
14. d
15. c

6. less
7. purchasing power parity
8. increase
9. falls
10. negatively

Fill In
1. fell
2. high
3. fall
4. surplus
5. supply of

Chapter 9

True/False
1. F, commercial paper is, for the most part, issued only by credit-worthy corporations
2. T
3. T
4. T
5. F, FDIC insurance is limited to $100,000 per account
6. T
7. T
8. F, MMMF stands for money market mutual funds (see Chapter 20)
9. T
10. T
11. F, MMMF business continues to grow
12. F, fed funds are reserves lent between member banks
13. F, see Drysdale Securities among others
14. T
15. T
16. T
17. F, noncompetitive bids simply take whatever return results from the auction process
18. F, Eurodollars are denominated in U.S. dollars
19. T
20. F, many nations, many currencies have money markets
21. F, MMMFs allow individual investors to participate in the money markets
22. F, MMMFs are not insured by the FDIC
23. T
24. F, Eurodollars are not confined to London banks

Multiple Choice
1. a
2. c
3. d
4. d
5. b
6. a
7. c
8. d
9. b
10. c
11. c
12. d
13. d
14. b
15. a

Fill In
1. Libor
2. money market mutual funds (MMMFs)
3. disintermediation
4. Treasury bills
5. reverse repurchase agreement
6. Treasury bills
7. below; discount
8. Negotiable CDs
9. Yankee
10. decline

Chapter 10

True/False
1. F, bonds are more likely to be called when interest rates fall
2. T
3. T
4. T
5. T
6. F, the after-tax return on the corporate (5.48%) is greater than the 5% return of the muni
7. T
8. T
9. T
10. T
11. T
12. F, convertible bonds can be converted into shares of common stock
13. T
14. T
15. T
16. F, Fannie Mae bonds have an implicit government guarantee making them almost free of default risk
17. F, ceteris paribus, a higher coupon bond will sell for a higher price
18. T
19. T
20. T
21. F, Treasury bonds are exposed to interest rate risk and purchasing power risk (inflation)
22. T
23. F, debenture bonds are not backed by collateral
24. F, indenture list the obligations of bond issuers

Multiple Choice
1. b
2. c
3. c
4. b
5. b
6. a
7. c
8. a
9. d
10. b
11. d
12. b
13. d
14. e
15. a
16. d
17. d

Fill In
1. fall
2. registered
3. junk
4. STRIPs
5. inflation indexed
6. general obligation
7. revenue
8. ten
9. Bulldog
10. yen

Chapter 11

True/False
1. F, the NYSE and the OTC markets are both part of the secondary market in stocks
2. T
3. T
4. F, such companies will have a great need for external capital to finance their growth
5. T
6. F, margin increases risk, and also increases potential reward
7. T
8. T
9. F, the DJIA has 30 stocks and is price weighted
10. T
11. T
12. F, non economic good sells for a negative price – the model just doesn't work when growth exceeds required return
13. F, the U.S economy suffered little harm, the Japanese economy suffered greatly
14. F, a raider needs common stock to gain voting control of the company
15. F, the facts indicate a risk-free rate of 3%
16. F, I just made up the term "equity default"
17. F, diversification exists when correlations are less than +1
18. T
19. F, I guess folks don't mind if the stock market goes *up* a lot, except for the short sellers
20. T
21. T
22. F, just one of those odd but true facts
23. T

Multiple Choice
1. c
2. c
3. d
4. a
5. c
6. a
7. b
8. a
9. b
10. a
11. a
12. a
13. d
14. b
15. d
16. d
17. d

Fill In
1. price weighted
2. New York Stock Exchange
3. circuit breakers
4. Philadelphia
5. specialist
6. price
7. value
8. dividends, growth, and required return on equity
9. ownership
10. designated order turnaround (DOT)

Chapter 12

True/False
1. T
2. F, mortgages do default and lenders do make great efforts to investigate the borrower's credit history
3. T
4. T
5. T
6. T
7. T
8. F, the guideline number is 36%
9. F, only Ginnie Mae bonds have an explicit guarantee
10. T
11. T
12. F, ARMs increase default risk, if interest rates go up it may become difficult for the borrower to make the increased payments
13. T
14. T
15. F, only Ginnie Mae bonds have an explicit guarantee
16. T
17. T
18. T
19. F, fixed rate payments won't change, but if interest rates go up it may become difficult for the variable rate borrower to make the increased payments
20. T
21. T

Multiple Choice
1. c
2. b
3. a
4. a
5. b
6. d
7. d
8. b
9. d
10. a
11. c
12. b
13. a
14. e
15. d
16. d
17. a

Fill In
1. increase; negative
2. greater than
3. reducing
4. falls
5. lien
6. debt-to-income
7. large
8. 36%
9. 80%
10. Amortization

Chapter 13

True/False
1. T
2. T
3. F, the U.S. did experience inflation under Bretton Woods
4. T
5. F, this is the job of the World Bank
6. T
7. F, the IMF is not part of the UN
8. F, the World bank is not part of the UN
9. F, the BIS is not part of the UN
10. T
11. T
12. F, the U.S. is a member of the BIS
13. F, World Bank bonds are highly rated
14. F, the IMF forced these nations to adopt contractionary policies
15. F, the number of interventions is higher than under Bretton Woods
16. F, several do
17. T (actually, the official currency is the Balboa, which is fixed at one Balboa to the dollar; however, I don't believe there are any Balboas in circulation and Panamanians use U.S. currency for daily transactions)
18. F, the Mexican peso is the currency of Mexico
19. T
20. F, such deficits did occur while the U.S. was on the gold standard
21. T

Multiple Choice
1. b
2. a
3. d
4. e
5. d
6. b
7. b
8. a
9. e
10. c
11. c
12. d
13. d
14. b
15. b
16. d
17. c
18. b

Fill In
1. World bank
2. World Bank
3. restrictive; reduce
4. the IMF
5. interest rate parity
6. BIS
7. declined
8. devalued
9. Bretton Woods Accord
10. Basel, Switzerland

Chapter 14

True/False
1. T
2. T
3. F, a bank run occurs when depositors attempt to withdraw all of their deposits prior to the bank failing
4. T
5. F, even the largest credit union is small compared to the money center banks
6. T
7. T
8. T
9. F, P&C insurers have greater liquidity needs than do pension funds
10. T
11. T
12. T
13. F, if the required reserve ratio is increased, the multiplier will become smaller
14. F, not quite *that* simple, not yet
15. T
16. T
17. T
18. T
19. F, the MB consists of total reserves plus currency
20. F, currency held by commercial banks is part of total reserves

Multiple Choice
1. b
2. b
3. a
4. a
5. d
6. c
7. a
8. d
9. d
10. d
11. b
12. d
13. c
14. c
15. b

5. credit union
6. lower than
7. finance company
8. corporate equities
9. Merrill Lynch
10. credit unions and pension funds

Fill In
1. multiple
2. federal government; states
3. checking deposits; loans
4. Certificates of deposit (CDs)

Chapter 15

True/False
1. F, Glass-Steagall was passed in 1933
2. F, the Glass-Steagall Act imposed this restriction
3. F, competition may have been the stated goal, but reality fell far short
4. T
5. F, even while so many banks were failing, there were few, if any, runs
6. T
7. T
8. F, reserve requirements are the same
9. T
10. F, this describes adverse selection
11. T
12. T
13. T
14. T
15. T
16. F, profits were quite high in the 1990s
17. F, the door swings both ways
18. T
19. T
20. T

Multiple Choice
1. e
2. e
3. a
4. b
5. d
6. d
7. c
8. c
9. e
10. d
11. a
12. b
13. a
14. d
15. b
16. d

Fill In
1. commercial bank
2. Great Depression
3. banking; capital
4. McFadden
5. multi-bank
6. financial holding company
7. fifteen
8. asymmetric information
9. Moral hazard
10. adverse selection

Chapter 16

True/False
1. T
2. T
3. T
4. F, many are chartered by the states
5. T
6. F, credit unions are not covered by FDIC, but are covered by NCUSIF
7. T
8. T
9. T
10. F, credit unions are allowed to make mortgage loans
11. F, the laws passed in the 1980s loosened S&L capital requirements and reduced restrictions on S&Ls
12. T
13. T
14. T
15. T
16. F, credit unions are regulated by the NCUA
17. F, savings banks and S&Ls are regulated by the OTS
18. T
19. T

Multiple Choice
1. c
2. d
3. b
4. a
5. d
6. d
7. b
8. c
9. a
10. d
11. d
12. d
13. b
14. d
15. b

5. credit union

Fill In
1. mutual
2. Savings Association Insurance Fund
3. share certificate
4. Central Liquidity Facility (CLF)

Chapter 17

True/False
1. F, GLBA asked the Fed to rely on the OCC, FDIC, or other regulators as much as possible, but did not eliminate Fed regulatory authority
2. F, the primary regulators of state chartered credit unions are the state banking commissioners
3. F, the primary regulator of nationally chartered credit unions is the NCUA
4. F, reserve requirements are set by the Federal Reserve
5. T
6. F, reserve requirements are set by the Federal Reserve
7. F, only $5,500,000 of core capital is required under the test
8. T
9. T
10. F, the FDIC still exists
11. F, the Federal Reserve is not subsidiary to the OTS
12. T
13. F, redlining refers to establishing geographic districts inside which a bank will make few, if any, loans
14. T
15. F, credit union deposits are insured by NCUSIF
16. F, PBGC regulates defined benefit pension plans
17. F, money markets are essentially unregulated
18. F, FIRREA represents re-=regulation
19. T
20. F, the FDIC is required to use the least costly method

Multiple Choice
1. a
2. d
3. a
4. d
5. d
6. b
7. d
8. d
9. a
10. a
11. a
12. b
13. c
14. c
15. b

Fill In
1. prior to
2. DIDMCA
3. Basel Accord
4. Securities and Exchange Commission
5. Federal Reserve
6. Office of Thrift Supervision
7. SEC
8. S&L crisis
9. twenty
10. financial holding company

Chapter 18

True/False
1. T
2. T
3. F, the fundamental principle is pooling of risk
4. T
5. F, income earned from investing the premiums stays with the insurance company
6. F, arson would be an example of moral hazard
7. F, an independent agent sells policies of several insurers
8. T
9. F, whole life premiums are generally paid periodically, although you can buy single payment insurance policies
10. T
11. F, a universal policy earns money market rates of return
12. T
13. F, this describes variable life
14. T
15. T
16. F, the insurance industry is regulated by the states
17. T
18. T
19. T
20. T

Multiple Choice
1. b
2. d
3. a
4. a
5. b
6. d
7. d
8. d
9. e
10. d
11. c
12. a
13. d
14. b
15. b
16. b

Fill In
1. Lloyd's
2. Adverse selection
3. moral hazard
4. actuarial or mortality
5. term; whole or permanent
6. equity
7. money market
8. life annuity
9. bankassurance
10. risk-averse

Chapter 19

True/False
1. F, Social Security covers workers, the self-employed, and their families
2. F, public pension funds account for about one-third of total pension fund assets
3. T
4. F, defined benefit plans are insured by the PBGC
5. F, defined contribution plans are faster growing
6. F, SIMPLE plans allow small business to offer pension plans
7. F, withdrawals from Roth IRAs are not taxed
8. F, most defined benefit plans are appropriately funded or underfunded
9. F, for employees, defined benefit plans have little investment risk
10. F, 401(k)s are extremely popular and most financial assets are eligible to be included in a 401(k)
11. T
12. T
13. T
14. T
15. F, 125% equity loans have high default risk
16. F, in non-contributory plans, the employee makes no contributions
17. F, a tax is a tax even if it is called a contribution
18. F, there will be two workers per retiree
19. T
20. T

Multiple Choice
1. b
2. e
3. b
4. c
5. c
6. a
7. b
8. d
9. e
10. d
11. a
12. a
13. b
14. c
15. c
16. d
17. c
18. d
19. b
20. b

Fill In
1. contributory
2. defined contribution
3. Keogh
4. traditional
5. $.1 trillion
6. Equities
7. 70+½
8. overfunded
9. Fidelity
10. 67

Chapter 20

True/False
1. T
2. T
3. T
4. F, they must register with the SEC
5. F, open-end companies do not trade on exchanges nor OTC; investors buy or sell directly from or to the open-end company itself
6. F, the SEC does not pass judgment on the economic merits of an offering
7. F, investors *must* be given a prospectus
8. T
9. T
10. F, most private placements are to insurance companies or pension plans
11. F, to sell short is to borrow *shares*, sell them, hoping to replace them by buying later at a lower price
12. F, open-end companies always trade at NAV (possibly plus a load)
13. F, balanced funds balance growth (equities) and income (bonds)
14. F, hedge funds are typically very risky
15. T
16. F, an aggressive growth fund would always be unlikely to own municipals, no exceptions
17. F, REITs invest in mortgages, not debentures
18. F, Fannie Mae and Freddie Mac are private corporations
19. T
20. F, Brokers make money through commissions, dealers make money from their bid-ask spreads

Multiple Choice
1. d
2. a
3. b
4. b
5. a
6. a
7. a
8. c
9. c
10. d
11. e
12. b
13. d
14. c
15. a

Fill In
1. primary; secondary
2. initial public offering (IPO)
3. seasoned offering
4. prospectus
5. indenture
6. day traders
7. net asset value (NAV)
8. half
9. diversification
10. Securities and Exchange Commission (SEC)

Chapter 21

True/False
1. T
2. F, in normal economic times interest rate spreads will be positive (the rates on mortgages will exceed the rates on passbook savings accounts, etc.)
3. F, capital refers to the amount of equity a borrower contributes
4. T
5. F, the larger the absolute value of the income gap, the more sensitive earnings will be
6. T
7. F, bank assets might default
8. T
9. T
10. T
11. T
12. T
13. F, duration gap measures the interest rate sensitivity of a bank's net worth
14. F, typically, ISAs < ISLs
15. T
16. T
17. T
18. T
19. F, if you expect interest rates to fall, you would want longer duration assets

Multiple Choice
1. d
2. b
3. b
4. b
5. c
6. d
7. b
8. a
9. a
10. b
11. a
12. c
13. c
14. b
15. b

Fill In
1. capital
2. capacity
3. assets
4. inversely
5. rise
6. insolvent
7. borrower
8. negative
9. positive
10. 125s

Chapter 22

True/False
1. F, only futures contracts have clearinghouses and margin
2. T
3. T
4. T
5. T
6. T
7. T
8. T
9. T
10. F, all three may be used to hedge or to speculate
11. F, futures contracts are marked-to-market
12. T
13. T
14. T
15. T
16. F, a call is more valuable if it has a lower strike price
17. T
18. F, options on more volatile assets have higher premiums
19. T
20. T

Multiple Choice
1. d
2. d
3. c
4. a
5. d
6. d
7. b
8. b
9. b
10. d
11. d
12. d
13. d
14. b
15. a

Fill In
1. put
2. sell (or deliver)
3. sell (or write) a call
4. standardized; customized
5. go long (buy)
6. margin
7. more
8. Chicago (CBOE)
9. Put
10. premium

Chapter 23

True/False
1. F, a cap provides the buyer with protection from higher rates
2. T
3. F, prepayments generally increase when interest rates decline
4. T
5. T
6. F, securitization has resulted in an increased supply of mortgages and other assets, reducing their interest rates
7. T
8. T
9. T
10. T
11. T
12. T
13. T
14. T
15. T

Multiple Choice
1. c
2. e
3. a
4. b
5. c
6. c
7. d
8. d
9. c
10. a

Fill In
1. liquidity
2. tranches
3. student loans
4. a cap and a floor
5. an interest rate swap
6. make payments to
7. net
8. two
9. floor
10. longer

Chapter 24

True/False
1. T
2. F, sustainable growth is along the long-term path
3. T
4. F, it is measured by real GDP
5. T
6. T
7. T
8. T
9. T
10. F, income taxes are based on nominal returns
11. F, the natural rate of unemployment is an economic construct defined as the unemployment rate which will trigger inflation should the unemployment rate fall below it
12. F, the more often used number is 3% not 2%
13. T
14. T
15. T

Multiple Choice
1. d
2. b
3. d
4. a
5. b
6. c
7. b
8. a
9. d
10. d

Fill In
1. price stability and sustainable economic growth
2. full employment; price stability
3. price stability
4. reduced (weakened)
5. fed funds
6. e-money
7. policy directive
8. buy
9. Sweep accounts
10. recognition lag, policy lag, and impact lag

Chapter 25

True/False
1. T
2. T
3. F, reductions in value are called devaluations
4. T
5. T
6. T
7. T
8. T
9. F, dollarization schemes are separate from currency boards
10. T
11. T
12. F, the European Central Bank will implement monetary policy in Europe
13. T
14. T

Multiple Choice
1. d
2. d
3. d
4. d
5. a
6. b
7. c
8. a
9. d

Fill In
1. devalue
2. Speculators
3. coordinate
4. rise
5. sell
6. sterilize
7. flexible
8. supply and demand